Scarred Hope
A Mother and Son Learn to Carry Grief and Live with Joy

authors
Beverly Ross
and
Josh Ross

Praise for
Scarred Hope

"When you go through something painful, you really want to hear from someone who has been there, done that (rather, *is doing* that). Beverly and Josh have been there. You have scars; they have scars. And they have a perspective that won't heal all your scars, but it will give you hope in spite of them. Let this book be the friend you're looking for."

--Ron L. Deal, bestselling family author, speaker, therapist, and grieving dad

"*Scarred Hope* is The Good Samaritan in book form. It extends a hand to the battered and broken, and offers each heart a safe place to rest, wrestle, question, and receive healing. Josh and Beverly welcome us into a powerfully raw account of how their own family tragedy gave birth to stubborn hope and courageous joy, offering practical truth and wisdom to readers all along the way. You will laugh, you will cry, you will jot down a million quotes, and then you will continue walking your own scarred story feeling freshly bandaged and incredibly hopeful."

-Sarah Brooks, Speaker, Storyteller and (inconsistent) blogger

"*Scarred Hope* is filled with the kind of deep truth a grieving person longs to hear- a truth you only understand when you have lived it. Beverly and Josh's honesty and vulnerability translates into something powerful and meaningful. Their words validate the pain a grieving person feels and often can't articulate. They offer practical steps forward and every word points to our only true hope- Jesus. This book promises to be a source of hope and healing for many."

Tami Glasco, Tara Farms Bed & Breakfast

"The loss of child is a journey that no one understands or wants to take. In *Scarred Hope*, Beverly and Josh articulate their spiritual journey in a way that makes the reader awaken to the profound emotional and spiritual transformation that takes place in those who grieve. When I began reading *Scarred Hope*, I did not want to stop. It is that compelling. I have walked with Beverly in her journey, and her authenticity and heart of compassion are revealed in *Scarred Hope*. Reading this book is almost as good as hearing Beverly speak in person."

Danny Mack, Director of Spiritual Life, Christian Care Communities and Services Mission and Development

"A friend once described grief to be like standing with your back to the ocean. You know a big wave is coming ashore, but you don't know when it's going to hit you. If you are standing on grief's shores or you want to stand in solidarity with someone who

is, this is just the book you need. My dear friends Beverly and Josh are trustworthy guides who can show you how hope can be re-birthed and joy can return."
Luke Norsworthy, Author, Podcaster, Preacher

"My wife Sharita and I live with grief like others live with some prized, expensive, heirloom chest of drawers in their homes. Grief is always there with us and there for us. Our grief is a chest of drawers shoved tight with individual grief, the grief we share as a couple and the grief we are honored to carry for others. Beverly and Josh's book *Scarred Hope* has helped us bring a great deal of order to the clutter of our drawers of grief. It is written from the depth of character both of them possess. So, their words are thoughtful, humorous, practical, and exude a warmth stoked by Christ's compassion. For those who are ready to take the necessary courage to sort out your collection of grief and grieving, allow these two trustworthy guides to get you where you need to go. Which is that sacred space and transformative place known as the presence of God."
Eric Leroy Wilson, Pastor, Author, Spiritual Director, and Poet
Sharita Wilson, Professor, Communication Specialist, and Motivational Speaker

"The story of my family and the Ross family spans three generations. Connected by the Holy Spirit through Christ's church, we have been witnesses to the activity of God in each other's family and ministry since 1969. I can imagine no greater heartache than losing a child or a sibling. All of us who have lost someone know the traveling companions of despair, longing, questioning, and emptiness that comprise what we collectively call "grief." And I cannot imagine many more truthful, honest, and God-honoring guides on the journey to healing than Beverly and Josh. *Scarred Hope* isn't a book. It's a gift. Beverly and Josh gift us the beauty of their story of grief and God while offering a compelling, meaningful, and honest path to handle the heartache and grief that inevitably visits our own stories."
Sean Palmer, author *40 Days of Being A Three* and *Unarmed Empire*, Teaching Pastor, Ecclesia Houston

"If you've never felt the sting of death or the crushing weight of grief, this book probably isn't for you. Through my own experiences of doubt and darkness, I've found Josh and his mother, Beverly, to be a guiding light on navigating seasons of grief. *Scarred Hope* is their sacred-ground story of God's faithfulness to a family in the midst of pain."
Justin Ardrey, Communication Minister, Sycamore View Church in Memphis, TN

"If you are a friend to someone who is experiencing grief and disappointment, I bet you are wondering what to say. Please don't let silence equal distance. Unexpected

loss may have created a chasm, but *Scarred Hope* can rebuild the bridge between your heart and theirs. And if you are the person who is experiencing grief and disappointment yourself, it can rebuild the bridge between your heart and God's."
Nika Maples, writer and speaker

"As Beverly and Josh share their hearts and story through *Scarred Hope*, they add validity to the grief process and offer blessings to bereaved children and their families. Thank you for using your personal story and journey and providing others with the gift of hope and healing! On behalf of many, thank you!"
Vicki Jay, CEO, National Alliance for Grieving Children

"The grief of others, like a pall, hangs over all our heads as well.
We go there, but are half afraid of those on whom the thunder fell."
-T.S. Eliot

In 1961, I was 24-years-old in my first full-time ministry at a little Mountain Village in Canada. Jesse and Ellen, in their 70s, spent their summers at their nearby lake cabin fishing, and encouraging Carolyn and me. Although Jesse had survived several heart attacks, they often took us fishing.

One afternoon Ellen called, from a city 100 miles away, in obvious distress. She had just received word that Jessie had been taken to the ER in our local hospital. She asked if I would I go be with Jesse until she got there. When I walked into Jessie's ER room, he said, in little more than a whisper, "Lynn, I'm not going to make it this time. Ellen is in Kamloops, today, so it will take her a while to get here."

I froze. I had no idea what to say or do. I panicked and tried, awkwardly, to assure him, "Naw, Jesse, you're going to be OK. We'll be out fishing again in a few days." Truth be told, I wanted to escape that room as fast as I could. But I held his hand briefly. Then after an awkward silence, I bowed my head and said a perfunctory prayer - and fled the room, leaving Jesse all alone.

By the time Ellen arrived Jesse was gone. And in the keening of her shock, I felt even more at a loss. That day I vowed to God that I would never again, God being my helper, leave another human being to die alone – or to grieve alone.

As I read this manuscript of this book, I couldn't help pondering how that long ago, dark afternoon could have been so much different for both Ellen and Jesse if I had

known then what is in this helpful book, *Scarred Hope,* by Beverly and Josh Ross. This book would have:
- kept me in the room with Jessie, listening while he spoke his heart.
- nurtured deeper empathy with the grief of others.
- supplied practical guidelines on what to say or not say; to do or not do in the presence of great grief.

If you are walking through deep grief or walking beside someone else who is grieving, *Scarred Hope* is the book for you.

    Lynn Anderson, author, pastor, and friend

To my five grandchildren:
Malaya, Jed, Truitt, Jocelyn, and Noah
You have filled my life with joy and light.
May you always cling to Hope, even when the path gets hard.
-Beverly

To my mom:
I know it's odd to dedicate a book to the person you co-wrote it with,
but Mom, I am honored to be your son.
Thank you for saying yes to this project.
More than that, thank you for saying yes to Jesus.
You have modeled courage in the face of uncertainty,
Bravery though there are reasons to be afraid,
And Hope no matter what comes our way.
I know Jesus better because of you.
Thank you.
-Josh

Contents

Foreword   Mike and Diane Cope

Introduction   Scars Come with Living

PART 1—Scars Tell Stories

Chapter 1   The February that Changed Everything
Chapter 2   The Loss of a Daughter; the Birth of an Anthem
Chapter 3   Does God Like Funerals?
Chapter 4   The Birth of Hope

PART 2—When Grief Moves In

Chapter 5   Grief as a Gift
Chapter 6   Grief as Common Language
Chapter 7   Grief as an Optometrist
Chapter 8   Grief as a Teacher
Chapter 9   Grief as a Friend of Joy

PART 3—10 Conversations

Chapter 10   Does time heal?
Chapter 11   Does everything happen for a reason?
Chapter 12   How many children do you have?
Chapter 13   Don't be sad; she's in a better place.
Chapter 14   How do you cultivate a healthy marriage while grieving?
Chapter 15   Should I seek help?
Chapter 16   Can Christians go to God angry?
Chapter 17   I know exactly how you feel?
Chapter 18   Does God cry?
Chapter 19   How can I be a faithful friend to someone who is grieving?

Epilogue   Stepping into the Arena

Acknowledgements

Foreword

"There were others."

We have always loved the raw honesty of the writer of Hebrews. Oh, sure: the Christian faith is filled with stories of people "who through faith conquered kingdoms, administered justice, and gained what was promised." There are thrilling narratives of those "who shut the mouths of lions, quenched the fury of the flames, and escaped the edge of the sword; whose weakness was turned to strength; and who became powerful in battle and routed foreign armies" (Hebrews 11:33-34).

But "there were others" (v. 35). The song of faith has a minor chord. It can even be a dirge. Sometimes we see desperate prayers answered; at other times, if feels like our prayers didn't make it above the ceiling.

But the "great cloud of witnesses" the writer speaks of (12:1) are those who pressed forward in faith, in anticipation, in joy. They didn't shrink back; they endured to the end.

In the midst of their suffering and endurance, they tasted the joy that is known only to those who have come to trust in God no matter what life brings. Henri Nouwen was right: "The cup of sorrow, inconceivable as it seems, is also the cup of joy. Only when we discover this in our own life can we consider drinking it."

We remember all too well the early weeks of 2010. We remember hearing about Jenny's illness, about her mysterious symptoms, about her turn toward serious complications. We remember calls and texts to Josh. Then we remember — with shallow breath because we had buried our own daughter — hearing that Jenny might not survive. And we also remember visiting with Beverly and Rick after she died.

It's a grief beyond grief. It's an unspeakable club (of parents who've lost children) that wishes it never had to "welcome" any new members. And yet, the Ross family, did, indeed, have to enter.

But they have pressed on with honest grief and gritty faith — along with sorrow and joy and questions and hope. Then, as so often happened, these "wounded healers" became guides to so many others.

There is no tip-toeing around the tragedy of loss in this memoir from Beverly Ross and Josh Ross. But in addition to the honesty about grief's gut-punch, it also offers a living witness to a life where the gospel and the believing community matter deeply.

-Mike and Diane Cope

Introduction
Scars Come with Living
(Josh)

"Josh, I have cancer."

It was a kick to the gut. I froze. My mind raced. All the what-ifs, whys, and this-isn't-fairs began playing in my head.

I was pacing a beach house condo with the cell phone to my ear. Kayci was on the couch waiting for a break in the storm so she could go back out to her sanctuary—the beach. She needs one beach trip per year. She doesn't want excursions, fun adventures, or planned activities. Kayci wants to lay out all day. Seriously. All day. Sunup to sundown. She may break for lunch. She may not. She considers it a spiritual gift.

The boys were in the back bedroom watching *Henry Danger*. They're always up for adventures, but since it was storming, they turned to devices to entertain them. Kayci and I sometimes have grand ideas about putting strict limitations on screen time for the boys. Yet, there are times we just cave. This was one of those days.

I was expecting a call from my mom that day while at the beach. We knew she had been to the doctor, that they ran tests, and that a call was coming. We just figured we knew how the call would go: "Hey Beverly, we saw the results from your tests. You're all good. Keep doing your thing."

Cancer doesn't run in our family. My great grandmother, Maw-Maw, died of cancer that grew in her mouth, but Maw-Maw was a chain smoker for over seventy years, and dipped much of that time too. She was what her generation called: a tomboy. In her late 80s, I witnessed her catch grasshoppers for fishing bait, ring the necks of chickens, and kill snakes. I watched from a distance. I was (and still am) as urban as you get. We thought she would live forever. Nicotine finally caught up to her.

Other than Maw-Maw, cancer hadn't intruded into our family history. In 2010, we had experienced tragedy with the sudden death of my sister, Jenny, but it wasn't cancer.

Immediately when you hear the "c" word, your mind is cluttered with questions and scenarios.

What if she has to have chemo?

What if she doesn't make it?

What if this is our last Christmas?

What if God doesn't heal her?

Why my mom?

We knew her diagnosis has a high survival rate, but the thought of poison being inside of your people is never calming.

Kayci and I cried. We shared the news with the boys. Then, I turned to comfort food: shrimp gumbo, a shrimp seafood platter, and extra jalapeno hushpuppies.

Ironically, we had to leave the beach a day early because a hurricane was approaching. Yet, a storm was brewing in our family too.

***

In moments of pain and confusion, I have to pause in order to remind myself of the foundation I have chosen to build my life on:

God created out of nothing in the very beginning. God still creates today.

God delivered in the Exodus. Jesus has brought the ultimate Exodus. God still delivers and liberates today.

God is full of steadfast love. This drives God more than anything else.

The tomb is empty. Jesus conquered death. The grave couldn't hold him, and for those in God, the grave can't hold us either.

God isn't just interested in lifting people out of pits and valleys. Through Jesus, God shows that He is willing to get down in the valleys with us. Incarnational living. God doesn't leave us alone in our pain. God is present on the journey.

I encourage people to think hard about the foundation they're building their lives on. If we wait until the storms of life hit to begin the process of building a foundation, it may be too late.

In prayer with God, while in the beach condo, I began rehearsing to myself truths about God's character, nature, mission, and purpose. I claimed them, confessed them, questioned them, and recited them. Over and over again.

I couldn't get past the question, "Why my mom?" So, I talked to God about it.

I got to a point in my faith a few years ago when I stopped comparing grief and pain to others. We hear it all the time. People choose to suppress, ignore, or minimize their own pain because there are others in the world who are worse off. And you know what? They're right. Yet, if God truly embodies the goodness of a loving, caring parent, God refuses to respond to our pain with, "Hey, be grateful. You could have it a lot worse." God's not too busy to give you His undivided attention.

I felt that while processing the news of my mom's diagnosis. Around the world that same day, people were receiving the news that their moms were terminally ill, or had inoperable tumors, or that they had suddenly passed. Yet, I didn't get the sense that God was minimizing my situation. God was on it. God cared.

But would God heal my mom? I didn't know.

God didn't heal Jenny. What if God didn't heal my mom either?

***

I'm assuming most of you have received similar phone calls like I did that day from my mom. I'm also assuming that you can remember where you were, what posture you were in, and the time of day. Grief does that kind of stuff to us. Grief takes mind-photographs and stores them in our memory.

The next day, we left Florida to make our way back to Memphis. We had to cut our beach trip short one day because the hurricane was approaching. The boys and I didn't mind; Kayci needed a therapist.

We stopped in Hattiesburg, Mississippi for the night. We checked into our hotel, and as we grabbed our bags to find our room, my cell rang. This time, it was my dad. My dad doesn't call much. We text. But we don't talk on the phone. My dad and my brother aren't phone talkers. They never have been. Sometimes I embrace it as a challenge to see if I can keep them on the phone longer than two minutes. Rarely am I successful.

So, when my dad calls, if I'm available, I answer. He doesn't call to shoot the breeze. He calls because there is something going on.

"Josh, I just got a call. You won't believe this, but your mom has been nominated for the Citizen of the Year award for Wise County. They want to keep it a surprise, but they're going to announce it next Saturday night."

Citizen of the Year!

That's kind of a big deal. Within two days, I received a call that my mom had cancer and a call that she was about to be named Citizen of the Year. She was being honored for her work with grief throughout the county.

As the boys swam at the hotel pool, I shared with Kayci the news about my mom's upcoming award. We were shocked, though we shouldn't have been. The impact of her counseling clinic and grief work could be felt in homes, schools, businesses, organizations, the local police department, and local churches. The county had never had a grief center before. With a growing staff and a vibrant vision, the clinic was making a real difference in people's lives throughout Wise County.

As a culture, we aren't good at grief. It makes us uncomfortable. We don't know how to give permission to grieve, so we try to rush through it. We don't know what to say when people are in deep pain, so we don't say anything. It's not that we wake up wanting to be cold, hard-hearted people; it's that many of us have never known of a way to embrace grief as a gift. My mom modeled this road through the death of her daughter - my sister - and then chose to invest her life equipping others for the journey they'll have to walk one day too.

"I should ask my mom to write a book with me." The thought came to me quickly, and I couldn't wait to share the idea with Kayci. She said we should go for it.

Later that day, I called my mom and asked if she would consider co-writing a book. I thought she may take a few days to let the fog settle on her health and then get back to me. But without hesitation, she said yes.

***

I often tell people that my dad taught me to love the Bible and my mom taught me how to pray. We didn't grow up as a wealthy family by our culture's standards, but we never knew it. Looking back, my parents made a lot of sacrifices for us. Most parents do for their kids.

My parents got married at 19, had a miscarriage at 20, and had my sister at 21. Jenny was born a few weeks after my dad graduated college, but my mom pushed pause on her degree to be a full-time mom. They had me at 23. I was born in Abilene, Texas, and they were waiting for me to be born to relocate to the Galveston area. My dad had a job waiting for him at Amoco Refinery. I was born in 1980, and my mom still reminds me annually that it is still one of the hottest summers on record.

In 1983, my little brother, Jonathan, was born, and that would be the final Ross child. Three was enough. My mom remained a stay-at-home mother until Jonathan started kindergarten. She chose to go back to school and complete her degree. She was a full-time mom during the day and a student at night. We never felt the impact. She was still joyfully present in our lives throughout that season. Occasionally, she'd have to go to school at night and dad would feed us McDonald's. Some might question if he loved us by feeding us McNuggets and Happy Meals. We thought he was awesome.

For the next decade of her life, my mom taught first grade and kindergarten. One year, the Mesquite ISD honored her with an award for being an outstanding educator. She poured her heart into the classroom, as she does with everything she is passionate about.

I sensed a shift in my mom's faith in the 1990s, around the time books like *Experiencing God* by Henry Blackaby were written, and her generation was introduced to the idea of having a relationship with God. I remember hearing her pray as a teenager and thinking to myself, "Whatever is in her, I want some of that." There was passion, courage, emotion, and relevance. Most of my life in church, prayers were stoic and void of bravery and joy. God used her to usher me into the deeper places of God's heart.

In her late 30s, my mom began teaching a Wednesday night class at our church. It quickly became a highly attended and anticipated event. A gift of teaching had emerged, and it's a gift that God has now used all over the country (and world). Looking back, it taught me about how spiritual gifts sometimes work. There are times a gift sits inside of someone for years (maybe decades), until the culture around them allows the gift to come to life. There are other times I think God holds off on dispensing spiritual gifts until we arrive at specific stages in our lives. I'm not sure which one happened with my mom, but it wasn't a gift that blossomed until her late 30s or early 40s.

It was around that same time that she sensed a new calling emerge in her life. She went back to school to get a master's degree in Marriage and Family Therapy. As we will share throughout this book, her practice has grown exponentially. The reason for the continued success of her counseling center is mostly this -- the way she (and my dad) have walked their own journey with grief has prepared them to guide others through theirs.

***

There are times in life when you get inducted into clubs you never signed up for and never intended to be a part of. No one looks forward to the day when they'll be divorced, have a miscarriage, lose a loved one, suffer injuries from a car accident, declare bankruptcy, or be diagnosed with cancer. Life is often like a game of cards; we're sometimes dealt a lousy hand. So, in life, it becomes a matter of what we're going to do with it. How are we going to choose to be faithful with the hand we've been dealt? We may not be able to control the outcome, but we can control how we choose to cling to hope, joy, adventure, and courage.

When I asked my mom about writing a book, the primary idea I had was to co-write a follow-up to my first book, *Scarred Faith*[1]. My mom was all about it.

The reality is that we all have scars. We have physical scars from falling off bikes, knee surgeries, c-sections, and accidents. Interestingly, every scar we bear has a story that goes with it. You'll never look in a mirror, see a scar, and think, "How in the world did that get there?" Each scar has a story. Our scars can be physical, and many are, but we also have scars that are social, emotional, psychological, and relational. It's a billion-dollar business to cover up scars. We do everything we can to hide them, suppress them, and pretend like they don't exist.

Yet, my mom and I believe that we're at our best when our scars become stories of redemption, hope, restoration, and courage.

A scar is a healed wound. Often, we don't ever let our wounds become scars because we keep picking at them. We don't give them time to properly heal.

Scarred Faith was my attempt to unpack tragedy, pain, suffering, and death. *Scarred Hope* is our attempt to continue the conversation.

---

[1] Josh Ross, *Scarred Faith*, (New York: Howard Books, 2013).

***

My mom and I are thrilled to take you on a three-part journey.

In *Part 1*, we're going to share pieces of our brokenness. Most of this section will be from my mom's perspective of losing a daughter and what has manifested since Jenny's death in 2010. We want you to know some of our own pain, as well as principles we have established to carry us through our own stories of grief. Pain can be redeemed. It may not be fixed, but it can be redeemed.

In *Part 2*, we discuss that grief is a gift. Grief doesn't go away. It takes on new shapes, sizes, and forms, but it never goes away. And we think this is a really good thing! We want to equip you to own your pain and grief. We hope to inspire you to use it to ignite adventurous, courageous living.

In *Part 3*, this is going to be really fun, and more importantly, helpful. My mom and I engage in ten conversations about suffering and pain. You get to pull up a chair and be a part of the conversation. This is going to be as practical as you can get. We want to use this section to serve you on your own journey, but to also prepare you to come alongside others in a way that helps them. It's too easy to hurt people with good intentions. We want to protect you from this.

I've attempted to limit how many times my mom can say "truth?!?!" (her way of asking for an "amen") and how many Brené Brown quotes she can use in this book. We'll see how it goes. I can't make any promises. And since she gave birth to me, she has the right to pretty much say whatever she wants.

We believe Jesus is greater than pain, cancer, heartache, depression, and death. These are all temporary. Hope is forever. Let's cling to it together.

Oh, and it's probably worth sharing that my mom writes this book as a woman who is cancer free. For that, we give thanks.

Chapter 1
The February that Changed Everything
(Beverly)

I do believe I have a story to tell. It's not the story I want to tell. It's not the story I ever dreamed of telling. But it's my story. I'd prefer to learn about hope through victory; not through pain, grief, and loss.

Can hope coexist with the darkness of devastating loss?

Rick and I stood at the foot of Jenny's bed on February 22, 2010. She is our firstborn. Our only daughter. I wanted to speak. My brain held an avalanche of words, not in the form of anything comprehensible. Thoughts were overwhelming my mind, racing faster than I could process them into words. I was desperate to get them out before I drowned in this torrential flood. I couldn't slow my mind to one thought though, it was like waves were rushing over me. Powerful, crushing, forceful waves.

***

My breath.

Where was my breath? I needed a breath. Just one breath. Our charge nurse walked over to us and my eyes locked with hers. For the first time since entering the hospital, I was speechless in her presence. No questions. No chit chat. No whispers about our faith.

I would have rejected any *answer* she would have spoken at this moment. I was not looking for cheap platitudes. *This story* was not going to end well. What words do you use when your precious daughter is losing her balance on the tightrope between life and death, falling towards death? What do you say when the worst of our fears is coming true? What words can possibly come to the surface in the screaming silence of this pain when the whole world doesn't make sense? It was our turn to have the worst day of our lives.

"I don't want to forget," I managed to say.

"You won't," she said, our eyes tightly locked.

"But I'm 52."

"You won't forget."

At this moment, there was nothing else more important than that. All those racing thoughts streamlined into one path: I didn't want to forget. I didn't want to forget the details of her life, her 31 years of life.

And I haven't forgotten much. I was afraid I would forget her voice, her smell, her smile, her eyes, her advice, her singing, her touch, her laugh, and her affirmation.

But I remember. I remember Jennifer Laine Ross Bizaillion. I remember the one we called Jenny, or JeJe. I remember her not only as my daughter, but as my friend and my teacher.

***

I was 21 when Jenny was born. I grew up right beside her. I didn't know my life without Jenny. I didn't want to know my life without Jenny. We loved shopping together. I bought lunch and the goodies; Jenny always bought a round of chocolate cookies at the kiosk. She taught me what was trendy in clothes and shoes, and she begged me to low-light my hair. Our conversations held space for the perfect blend of laughter and depth. The discussions included stories about the generations behind me and dreams for the generations in front of her.

Jenny and I had spent so much time together. And now, here we were, in Baylor Grapevine ICU, saying goodbye.

I am going to tell you the story of her death, but this isn't the best part of Jenny. The pain rarely is the best part. The best parts are usually the stories on either side of the deep, piercing wounds that one day form scars. The stories before the wound are what give it a high price tag and a searing pain. The stories that form after the initial wound, the raw gaping wound, delicately hold the sacred space as we explore how to get back up, how to walk again, and figuring out if getting back up even matters anymore.

Depending on the depth of the wound, we will forever define our lives by the before and after of the onset of pain. Details fit together to plot out the direction of each step we will take for the rest of our lives. And I have come to believe that **direction is everything.** The process became more important than speed. If I'm being really honest here - which my commitment to you is to speak with as much honesty as I know throughout this book -- I had to reaffirm my life's destination. I had to learn to commit. Again.

Whew. Deep breath. Buckle up. Hold on tight. Here's the story.

***

In January 2010, my husband, Rick, and I stood in our kitchen more than once, saying to each other, "Does life get better than this?" We were coming off of a joy-filled Christmas season with our family gathered at our house. We had lots of laughter and deep conversations. Everything felt so complete.

Our kids married people that we absolutely adore. When they were growing up, I taught them the way to great happiness was to marry someone sold out to Jesus, and someone I liked. Of course, the Jesus part was of utmost importance, but I made sure they knew that the "I liked" part is to never be forgotten or minimized. All three of my children believed me and married people we adore.

All three families were serving the Lord in powerful ministries. Jenny was helping lead an international children's ministry, KidStand, with her best friend, Jessie Beebe. Josh was pastoring a church in Memphis, Tennessee. Jonathan was the worship pastor for a church in Houston, Texas. My heart was filled to overflowing!

When the kids were in those rocky teen years, my heart cry was, "My dear children, for whom I am again in the pains of childbirth until Christ is formed in you."[2] But after they were adults, I often found myself reciting, "I have no greater joy than to hear that my children are walking in the truth."[3]

Rick and I were both involved in ministries that reached beyond anything we would've dared to dream. Rick was (and is) the pastor of a church that we love. I had recently opened a nonprofit counseling practice, Wise County Christian Counseling, in our community and it was absolutely thriving. One of my favorite phrases for this season was, "I *love* my life!" and it was always spoken with great enthusiasm and a sassy movement of my head!

One of the things I loved about my life was my calling to be a speaker. I loved blending my faith and career to offer words of healing and hope to people in pain. I focused on bringing words that would help all of us prepare in the Light for what we will do when darkness came.

---

[2] Galatians 4:19.
[3] 3 John 4.

It seems right to say that again: *Prepare in the Light for what you will do when darkness comes.*

***

At the end of January, I was scheduled to fly to San Antonio to speak at a women's event. It was SAN ANTONIO! Anytime I receive an opportunity to speak in the city that gave us Mi Tierra and that flows with authentic Mexican food, I receive it as a calling from God that must be answered. I was scheduled to speak on Ephesians, probably my favorite book in the Bible. I couldn't wait to share about knowing our God-given identity so we can walk out healthy relationships with each other, and to stand firm in the Lord when the way gets dark. Little did I know that the message I had prepared to give to others is what I was going to need for my own soul as I walked the undesired road of suffering that was soon to unfold.

Early Saturday, January 30, before my speaking event started, Jenny texted me to say she wasn't feeling well. I called her, but she didn't answer. She texted back to tell me that her throat was sore, and she didn't have a voice. She went on to Malaya's basketball game, coughing all through the video she made for us.

Jenny went to the doctor on Monday, February 1, and was diagnosed with the flu, which was an epidemic in the Dallas-Fort Worth area. She was given Tamiflu and sent home to recover. She didn't get better on Tuesday or Wednesday.

Thursday morning, February 4, David texted me early and said they were in the doctor's parking lot waiting for them to unlock the doors. Jenny was worse. I hurriedly dressed and loaded up a backpack with books on marriage. Oh, the hubbub created by Valentine's Day! I was scheduled to speak at three marriage events during the month of February, and I would use this time to prepare.

David called to tell us they were sending Jenny to Baylor Grapevine Hospital for fluids. She was dehydrated. Rick and I rerouted and headed that direction. I looked forward to sitting with her while she was receiving an IV. We hadn't had much chance to visit since the Christmas holidays and I wanted to catch up. I knew she was thinking about going back to college and I wanted to hear every detail. I wanted to hear the excitement in her voice as she shared her dreams for the future.

Rick and I walked into the emergency room where several nurses surrounded Jenny. She had an oxygen mask on. Our eyes locked. I'm not sure if it was fear in hers but I know it was fear in mine. I turned around and saw Malaya, our 9-year-old granddaughter, and her eyes were filled with terror. Rick got her out of the room immediately.

A doctor asked David and me to step out into the hallway where she put up the x-ray images of Jenny's lungs. She said, "We have a 60/40 chance." I looked at David for a clue.

"A 60/40 chance of *what*?"

The doctor turned around and looked at me with a mix of kindness and firmness, "Of life. Your daughter is really sick. One of her lungs is 100 percent filled with fluid. The other is 75 percent filled." They were admitting Jenny, taking her to an isolation room in ICU until they could figure out what was attacking her body.

We were instructed to meet Jenny upstairs. As soon as we stepped into the corridor to the isolation unit, her nurse asked me if I would answer some questions about Jenny's health history. Well, of course, I could. I knew her longer than anyone. She spoke her first words very young and walked early. She struggled with kidney infections as a toddler but outgrew them by the time she was six. She was allergic to cats and had seasonal allergies, but overall, really healthy.

I sat down at a computer with him and began to answer all the trivia that makes up one's medical history. I kept glancing around trying to figure out what was going on in Jenny's room. I knew I had to do this *facts* part, but my heart was desperate to get in the room with her. My world was spinning faster than I could assimilate the thoughts, but somehow, it felt like a horrible game of Freeze Tag. Somebody needed to touch me so I could run.

***

This scene at a nurse's desk while Jenny was being cared for in another room seemed familiar. It *was* familiar. I had been in this position before.

In 1981, when Jenny was three, we were celebrating Thanksgiving with Rick's family on Lake Tawakoni. Jenny and her young cousin burst into the back room where I was tending to Josh, who was a baby. They wanted to go see the lake. I asked Rick's brother to go with them and he agreed. As I was finishing with Josh, I heard my brother-in-law's voice, so I asked about the kids. He shrugged. He had left them at the lake telling them not to go any closer. With none of his own, he didn't know children, and he really didn't know 3-year-olds. I went running, still holding Josh.

I didn't see Jenny, only her cousin standing on the dock. Where was Jenny? No one knew where she was. Her cousin had a look of panic on his 3-year-old face, and we knew something was horribly wrong.

I began to beg the Lord to help us find her. I was terrified she had been kidnapped. It was on every parent's mind. We were living in the midst of the Adam Walsh stories.

Somebody yelled, "There she is!"

"Yes, Lord! Thank you!" I said in my spirit.

She was facedown in the water.

"Please, Lord, let her be alive!"

Rick's brother jumped in, grabbed her, and yelled, "She's alive!"

"Yes, Lord! Yes!"

He heard her cough. I knew that didn't necessarily mean life.

"Please, Lord, help her to be really alive!"

He passed her limp body to a man walking down the private road who said he knew CPR.

She coughed more and moaned.

She was really alive!

"Oh Lord, You are the Miracle Worker. You heard my cries for help!"

I rode in the ambulance taking Jenny to Children's Hospital in Dallas, singing every song we knew. I couldn't bear to let Jenny out of my sight, but when we arrived, the paramedics whisked her off to be examined, as I was forced into a line to complete the paperwork for insurance and payment. When I finally got that completed, I ran upstairs to her room where I was stopped for the second time to answer questions about her medical history. When I got there, she was begging a nurse to stop something - I'm not sure what - but I couldn't leave until I answered every question. I stood there because I truly believed that my answers would help the doctors find the best treatment for our Jenny.

***

Twenty-nine years after the terrifying lake incident, I was once again having to recall Jenny's medical history. The Lord was going to heal Jenny just like He had when she was three. Then, we had been deeply grateful that the Lord had heard our cries and healed our precious daughter. And now, God was going to do it again, right?

That time, in 1981, her lungs were clear. The temperature was cold, and since she was so young, the mammalian reflex had taken over and prohibited water from getting in her lungs. After spending one night in Children's Hospital for observation, we headed home. She would be okay.

This story is a vital part of my testimony. That day the Lord taught me about prayer. It was a day I felt so loved by Him. It was the day He introduced Himself to me as not only *the* Miracle Worker, but *my* Miracle Worker.

***

I stepped into the isolation room with Jenny. She pulled the oxygen mask down, "Mom, I can't believe I'm this sick."

"You are," I conceded. "But we are in a really great place. We are going to get this figured out." I spoke those words with clarity, conviction, and full of hope. I was confident that the Lord would do it again.

The ending of a story determines the tone for the retelling of it. This is true for every path that generates brokenness. Whether it is marital struggles or depression, car accidents, miscarriages, or cancer, the ending of the story determines how we retell it. These exact same scenes would have a different voice and color if the ending were different. I wanted this story to end with the same excitement as the story of 1981. But, it didn't.

Dr. Lester, our hospitalist, joined us at Jenny's bedside. "Jenny is the sickest person in ICU." My first thought was that he had to be exaggerating. I started to smile but the look in his eyes said it was raw truth. Jenny was really sick. Over the next few weeks, we became familiar with Dr. Lester's firm honesty and his tender compassion.

Jenny was awake and talked some. She removed her oxygen mask to instruct us who to call to get her make-up and find her contacts. She asked me to wash her back off. She sat up and I found a wet cloth. I wish I would've lingered a bit longer. Just a little bit longer. I had no clue, no clue the terror that was coming.

When Dr. Kollipara, the critical care specialist assigned to us, entered the room, I felt a rush of relief. He was the epitome of confidence, exhibiting a sacred mix of compassion and medical knowledge. The nurses adored him, and they reassured us how grateful we should be to have him caring for Jenny.

Dr. Lester and Dr. Kollipara were an amazing team and worked beautifully in sync with each other, and with us. I've heard of "white coat syndrome" negatively affecting people. These two white coats had the total opposite effect on us. They filled us with confidence for this fight.

Dr. Kollipara's first task was to figure out what was wrong with Jenny. Her symptoms were not typical of the flu. He began to prioritize the order of testing and care. A tech came in to take blood to check her oxygen saturation levels. It was incredibly painful for Jenny. Our eyes were locked, without spoken words, but with the deep connection that most mothers and daughters share on a visceral level.

From the earliest test, Dr. Kollipara reported to us that Jenny never had the flu. She had Group A Strep that had gone without an antibiotic. His said, "The wimpiest of antibiotics would have wiped this out." Now, our precious daughter was septic. Her organs were shutting down. It was too strange and too complicated to even predict how this happened.

Jenny had an empyema (a collection of fluid outside the lung) which required immediate draining. Empyemas are quite painful and can make breathing difficult. When the doctor came in to drain it, they had me step out, but I was looking through a window from the nurse's station. I saw Jenny sit straight up as she fought for air. She was intubated immediately.

What on earth was happening? That small tube would prohibit us from hearing her voice. Oh, my ears ached to hear her voice. But if that tube would aid in Jenny's healing, I was all for it. I could go a little while without hearing her. But not forever. *Please don't ask me to go for the rest of my time on earth without hearing her.*

Our first night-shift nurse was so wonderful to us. David and I stayed in Jenny's room, dozing off and on, but frequently waking with a startle. With every glance at the monitor, we bore witness to the fight for life.

Each time our nurse came in to check on Jenny, I would ask, "Is there hope?" She would respond by giving us a thumbs up. We still call her our "thumbs up" nurse. Hope was alive in that room! (A couple of years later, she gave us a statue of a thumbs up that I keep in a special place in my office. We call it The Thumb of Hope.)

Our sons, Josh and Jonathan, came in on Jenny's second day in the hospital. Rick and I hated for them to see their sister like this - so many tubes, unable to communicate, fighting for life. As much as I hated for them to see her so sick, I knew there was nothing that I could do to protect them. This was really happening. We were forced to go through this together.

The boys became our protectors. They sat on the floor with me while I cried, one on either side of me. They tucked me under a desk when I had gone too long without eating but still wanted to visit with friends in the waiting room. Josh put a piece of pizza in my hand and moved my arm so I would take a bite. Jonathan found a video of Alicia Keyes singing "Empire State of Mind" and played it for me. It was a good distraction from the mounting fear.

Friends and family gathered to encourage us, sit with us, pray with us, and to feed us. As the crowd became larger, hospital security came to visit us. They said it looked more like a cafeteria buffet line than an ICU waiting room. Security said the crowd size might intimidate the other patient's families. These people gathered to remind us that we were not alone. How could we ask them to leave?

Even after Jonathan made the announcement under the security's watchful eye, our friends didn't go far. They left the ICU waiting area to disperse to every other waiting room they could find, and some created waiting rooms out of nooks and crannies in the halls. Every time we received any news or reports from a doctor, there were runners that would go from group to group. The energy poured into our family was invigorating. Hope was alive in this place!

Our friends anticipated our every need. They brought blankets, lip gloss, books, games, and prayer crosses (the kind that are easy to cling to tightly when you pray). They delivered snacks, coffee, and ice chests of drinks. One friend wanted to buy a small refrigerator. We begged her not to do that in our fear of upsetting security again.

The janitor in the waiting room spoke limited English but we often shared tender smiles. One morning, she came over to me, hand outstretched with the best gift she had to offer. "For you," she said as our eyes met. It was my very own personal roll of toilet paper. How sacred was the connection - over toilet paper.

A CarePage was created and prayer warriors began to write in to speak words of life, encouragement, and strong hope. Jenny had a passion -- I mean a deep, urgent passion -- for unity in the Body of Christ, and these CarePages were evidence of the body of Christ uniting. The walls between churches did not exist as we were joining hands and hearts to pray for Jenny's healing. I just knew she and I were going to discuss the joy found in this unity one day soon.

In addition to our two lead doctors, we had a doctor for almost every single body part. A nephrologist, a kidney specialist, woke us up on our first Monday, February 8, with the news that Jenny needed to have surgery on her kidneys, but that it was unlikely that she would survive it.

Wait a minute! Let's start this over. Who are you and repeat all that again?

Dr. Kollipara came by within the hour. We were all in Jenny's room, and he kept looking into my eyes. "What is wrong?" Still trying to digest the wakeup call and process the information, I only nodded my head "no." My throat was closing again. Tears were gathering to form a rushing flood. He said, "Has someone said something?" I nodded in affirmation. "I can't help you if you don't tell me." That's all I needed. I'm sure he knew exactly what had happened. He looked at me intensely, our eyes locked. "You are going to have a lot of doctors come in and out of here. Every doctor thinks their body part is the most important to sustain life. I am the doctor looking at the whole body. You listen only to me. Jenny isn't having kidney surgery right now. You have got to tell me when people say things so I can help you understand."

Before this day was over, we had two other scary brushes with death. Our doctors wanted to try a risky drug that could be a turning point, hopefully, a turn toward health. Within a few hours on it, Jenny started to bleed. I asked our nurse, "Is this it?" She said, "It could be." No! She ordered more blood and things calmed quickly.

That night it looked like something was wrong with Jenny's gallbladder. We asked for prayers. A surgeon came and found nothing wrong with her gallbladder. The doctors wanted a CT scan of Jenny's body to explore why she wasn't improving. That meant taking her off her vent and using a bag to force air into her lungs. They shared the risks with us. The elevator was the worst part. If something went wrong on the elevator, help could not get to her fast enough.

It was after midnight. Prayer warriors assembled around us. People paced. Some laid face down on the floor. Some quietly whispered in corners. I stood at the door, facing the elevators, looking through a little window. The doctors stepped out first, their white coats flying as they danced in circles and high-fived each other. They had made it! Jenny was wheeled out of the elevator! She made it and nothing new showed on the scan.

This day once again reminded me of 1981. We prayed. The Lord answered.

CHAPTER 2
The Loss of a Daughter; the Birth of an Anthem
(Beverly)

Jenny spent those first hyper-critical days in an ICU isolation room, with one nurse whose only task was to care for her. I rarely left her room. David sat for hours at Jenny's bed and read all the FaceBook and text messages to her, stroking her hair and face. Someone brought an iPod (remember those?) and a speaker to Jenny's room. Worship music played nonstop. Jenny loved music. Some of those songs became my favorites. Some are too hard to hear again. *Mighty to Save* was one the songs that comforted us and it was chosen as the sign-off on our CarePages. We knew God could save her life, and everything in us was trusting Him to do it.

The words of the song *Mighty to Save* come from Zephaniah 3:17, "The LORD your God is with you, He is mighty to save. He will take great delight in you, He will quiet you with His love, He will rejoice over you with singing." We knew God wasn't a genie or a Santa Clause kind of God. We already knew that some things happen while our feet walk on dirt that break His heart too. But we knew He **could** do it. With any movement of His eyelash, He could save Jenny's life and restore her health. We knew her organs could wake up with a twitch of His pinkie. We begged Him to do just that.

"Move, Lord, please move. Just like You parted the water to save the Israelites, we believe You can part the flood of this terror. We believe You can give us dry land. We believe in You, Lord. You are mighty to save. You are, Lord. You can do this."

***

I felt like I was being beaten with a baseball bat in places I didn't even know I had. The wounds were deep, and my heart was cringing with every blow. Confusion was swirling all around me but didn't compare to the tornado in my spirit. I was clinging to Hope.

A few days in, as soon as she was stable enough, Jenny was moved out of isolation to a regular ICU room. She still had one nurse assigned to her. (Most of the nurses work with two patients at a time.) That was a continued indication of how sick she was. But the doctors and nurses also were using the phrase, "She's trending well."

The Lord continued to reveal Himself through His people. Dear friends handed us a hotel key so we could get better rest. Rick and I were at the hotel sleeping when my cell phone rang in the middle of the night. We jumped to alertness. The nurse said Dr. Kollipara was in Jenny's room to try to wean her off the vent. He wanted us to come in case it scared her. We ran to the car. The ventilator was the *thing* between her voice and our ears. When we got there, Jenny was back asleep. Her body wouldn't cooperate, but Dr. Kollipara said she never looked scared. I believed him.

***

On February 15, Rick dropped me off at the hospital and was headed back to Decatur to spend some time in the office. David was going to catch up on some work before joining me. When I walked back to check on Jenny, our nurse told me that an orthopedic surgeon had been by and was scheduling Jenny for leg amputations that afternoon. We knew her extremities, her fingers, her legs, even her ears, were turning black. When your body is fighting for life, all the circulation goes to the vital organs. The meds were also focusing attention on her core, her trunk. But this? No one had discussed amputations with us. I asked our nurse to call Dr. Kollipara immediately. I couldn't reach Rick or David. I was alone and was forced to trust the process. Dr. Kollipara was able to slow things down a bit. He wasn't sure the timing was right for amputations.

The morning of February 17, Dr. Kollipara and Dr. Lester called all of us -- Rick, David, Josh, Jonathan, and me into a family room. It was time. Amputations of both legs needed to happen soon. The black, dry gangrene was moving up her legs towards her knees. It would be easier for Jenny to adjust to prosthetics that were below the knee. We made the decision to do it. What a heartbreaking life-changing decision to make for someone else. I remember feeling the weightiness of the choice we'd made, but trusted our doctors to lead us. We were willing to do whatever needed to be done to save Jenny's life. We wanted her home with us. I remember telling the doctors that I wanted her heart.

I began to plan how I was going to teach her to walk again. Little did I know at the time that I would be the one who would have to learn to walk again.

Here we were again. Terror was moving in close. But we felt surrounded and protected by the people gathering around us and those writing in on our CarePage, all of us tightly bonding with our eyes on Jenny. We had one purpose - to sustain her life. Some people knew her. Some people knew us. Some people knew of a young woman struggling. Some knew of a family struggling. All were praying with one heart and one voice, "Lord, please save Jenny."

After the surgery was completed, we felt a sigh of relief. Maybe now she could begin to heal. Her vitals still appeared to be trending well. She wasn't getting worse, and some organ functions began to show baby steps toward progress.

***

Oh, Jenny!

My first memories of you involve your feet. I had one of them stuck under my ribs late in pregnancy. I would rub your heel and be so thankful that I could carry you in my womb. I had a C-section after a long labor to birth you. My hands were strapped down during the surgery, but the moment you were in our pediatrician's arms, he brought you to me and held you so that I could touch your precious foot. That heel! I fell in love with you with that one little touch of your heel.

I loved the recording you and Jonathan did for his wedding, Twila Paris's "How Beautiful." Some of the words you sang were from Isaiah, "How beautiful are the feet that bring good news."[4] You, my daughter, brought the best news of all to so many hurting hearts. You brought the news of Jesus! By your feet, many came to know Him.

Now, those beautiful feet were gone. But it seemed total silliness to grieve for your feet when their loss meant we could have your beating heart. People began to offer advice about prosthetics. We committed to making sure you had the very best.

With your amputations came a tracheotomy. Your ventilator tube had been in long enough.
Your room became eerily quiet, except for the monitor. It was the monitor that showed your heartbeat, your blood pressure, and the rate of your breath.

You still had one nurse at all times. Oh, the nurses! They became some of my closest friends. When you walk that kind of depth with people, the connection becomes impenetrable. When you watch people care for your special person in ways that you can't, you just love them.

You didn't seem to be in pain, but you did start running a fever. Your liver wasn't healthy enough for you to have medication to bring your temperature down, so they used ice and a fan. You tried to talk to Dad once. We weren't sure if you asked about Malaya or your legs. Surely you can see how we got confused. I wanted to be one of

---

[4] Isaiah 52.7.

those intuitive moms that understood what you were saying, but I never could get it. Please don't forget what it was and tell me when we see each other again, okay?

***

February 20 brought a new dimension to the level of terror. It was a Saturday morning. David called as we were getting ready to head to the hospital. Our nurse had just called to tell him, through her tears, that Jenny had started having seizures. Her words, "I'm sorry." That couldn't be remotely okay.

I don't think I've ever seen anything harder to witness than a seizure. Our day nurse would keep the meds in her pocket to stop them, and when one would begin, she would get between me and Jenny and whisper calming words to her until the horribly frightening event stopped. Her voice spoke the words I wanted to speak.

Dr. Lester came in and told us they needed to find the cause. When the tests were over and the results in, he took David, Rick, and me into a back room where we could view the images of her brain. The lesions were small but scattered. Some of the lesions were near her sight center. A new level of terror opened up right there in that tiny room. Just when I thought the fear was as deep as it could go, the floor moved and there was a new level.

I was back and forth a lot the next two days, from the waiting room to Jenny's room. I didn't know what to do with myself. The seizures were impossible to watch, but the waiting room seemed too far away from Jenny.

***

Monday morning, February 22, all was quiet at the hospital. The seizures were continuing, not worse, but still randomly present. Mid-morning, some friends began to trickle in to sit with us. There was a weird feeling in Jenny's room. I couldn't shake it. I went to find our charge nurse twice to tell her something was wrong. I wasn't sure what, but I knew something wasn't right. We had a new nurse for that day. Maybe that was it. We hadn't had a new nurse in what seemed like forever. I knew it had only been 18 days but sometimes the clock doesn't reflect time well. If you've had a season of pain, you know exactly what I'm talking about here. There was an intense unsettling.

The infectious disease doctor came in to rearrange some of Jenny's medications. He looked at me and at Rick saying, "Don't give up hope. We are going to be able to figure this out." I replied with conviction, "I am not giving up. I have hope. I have so much hope."

I stepped back into the waiting room to catch a breath. One of my mentors was walking in. I hadn't seen her in years. She had encouraged me when I was a struggling young pastor's wife, and I was always delighted to spend time with her. I jumped up to hug her, but as I wrapped my arms around her, I felt this magnetic pull, an overpowering magnetic draw to get back to Jenny. I ran.

When I opened the door to the ICU, my eyes met our nurse's eyes. She was on the phone with an intense look and said, "Jenny has plummeted." That's all I heard. I know she said more words, but that's all I heard. They were going to take her for a brain scan. My physical reaction was to both freeze and run at the same time.

David, Rick, and I had a deal that if we ever needed help when one of us was with Jenny we would text one letter and the others would come immediately. But I had left my phone in the waiting room. I ran to get Rick. When I opened the door to the waiting room, David was walking in too. "Jenny has plummeted. Something is wrong." We all ran back to be with Jenny. Oh, God, please. Please. Please, help us.

Our charge nurse was in Jenny's room now. The connection with her was and continues to be so thick. Early on, she had told me that she was a believer in Jesus too. We shared something sacredly sweet.

The three of us stood around Jenny. Our charge nurse lowered the railings on her bed, eyes locked on mine. As I search through my mind, I can't remember her next words. But we knew we were telling Jenny goodbye.

"What if it's too early?"

"Do it anyway," she said.

Wait a minute. Is this for the test or for life? I wanted it to be for the test. Everything in me wanted it to be for the test. I think she knew it was for life.

I told Jenny we would be okay. I told her that we would take care of Malaya. I reassured her that we would point Malaya to Jesus. All my senses were lighting up in total terror. No! This was not okay. Nothing about this was okay. *How, Lord? How many prayers does it take? Was there a formula I missed?*

Some of the next few hours are deeply etched in my heart. Some aren't there at all. They are totally gone. I either totally remember it, or I have no memory of it at all.

I don't remember them taking Jenny for the test. I don't remember them rolling her back into her room. I do remember not long after she was back in her room, Dr. Lester and Dr. Kollipara pushed through the doors with force and purpose. *Yes, here they come. They will help us.* I remember their serious faces and fast steps to get to Jenny. I remember Dr. Kollipara's white coat open and blowing in the wind that his quickness created. I remember him saying that he was going to call UT Southwestern. Yes, a new idea to help us. I saw Dr. Lester's eyes meet Dr. Kollipara's eyes and the intensity made my heart feel nauseated, absolutely sick. The two doctors went to Jenny's bed, closing the curtain around the three of them. It was the first time we had been on the other side of the curtain.

Oh God, now would be perfect timing for one of Your miracles! We know You can, and we have trusted, with everything in us, that You would.

I remember staring at the white curtain. I wanted to see what was going on. I wanted to hear what was happening. *Not this, Lord. I don't want to see this or hear the words that were about to come.*

As we were sitting in the hall outside Jenny's room, there was a family in the room next door to Jenny's staring at us with fear in their eyes. Their teenage son was sitting up in bed. I never got a chance to meet this family or offer words of encouragement. I was surprised at the shame coming up in me; shame that my presence was creating such pain. I didn't want this to be part of my story. The nurses began to set up curtains around us to serve as a barrier from the other ICU families. Oh, the curtains of death!. We had seen them before. I did not want to be behind them.

The doctors came out and said that we needed to find a place to talk. To get to the family room meant we would have to walk through the waiting room. The waiting room was filling up with people who love us. I couldn't face them yet. We were following Dr. Kollipara. He stopped before opening the door to the waiting room.

"Stay right behind me."

I was determined not to look anywhere but at him. I didn't know what was happening yet, and I certainly didn't want to attempt to explain it to anyone else. I didn't look over at our friends and family. I could feel their presence and my heart flooded with gratitude that they were close. As we walked by, their chatter hushed, and silence fell over the entire room. This was a horrible thing that was happening, and our friends were there to stand with us.

If I had glanced once at that crowd, I would've melted into their collective arms. I never would've made it to that room where we would talk about the next steps, the steps I never wanted to take, the steps I had tried hard to avoid.

When the door to that room closed, I laid my head back on a couch. Staring at the ceiling, I asked, "What next? Just tell us what to do." Dr. Kollipara began to speak. He was so kind and so heartbroken, as was Dr. Lester. This was not the way any of us wanted this story to end. They asked us not to stay in while they pulled Jenny off life-support. They explained that the human body can have some involuntary movements that could be hard to watch. We agreed. They said we could go in one more time before they removed the machines.

David, Rick, and I walked back into her room. We were joined by a very small group of friends and family. The room was so quiet except for a few quiet sobs. I do not remember doing this, but our precious charge nurse told me two weeks later that I started praying at this point. I asked if she could remember anything I said. She said I started by saying, "I am so confused. This is not what we wanted to happen. We don't know how to walk this road. I don't even know my life without Jenny. I grew up beside her. But I do know this: I know that I don't want to walk away from You because of this." Then she said that I opened my eyes and with great resolve said something like, "I want each of you to promise me that you will not walk away from faith because of this moment. Promise me." She said that I went person to person waiting for a response. There were 11 of us in that room and I made each person pledge to me, even our nurse, that they would not walk away from faith because of Jenny's death.

***

Remember that backpack I had brought to the hospital? One of the books in it was my Bible. I couldn't read one word from any book, including my Bible. I am grateful that I had some verses written on the walls of my heart for such a time as this. One was Isaiah 45:3. It is the Lord speaking, "I will give you the treasures of darkness, riches stored in secret places that you may know that I am the Lord your God, who calls you by name." It doesn't say that the Lord gives darkness, but rather that He lets us find treasure in it. The other is where this prayer comes from (Daniel 3:17, paraphrased by me): "Our God is able to save us. But even if He doesn't, we will NEVER serve another." We call that a no-matter-what-kind-of faith.

***

We left Jenny's room and went to wait. We found out at a visit two weeks later that both our doctors stayed with Jenny until it was over, and that Dr. Lester sang "It Is Well with my Soul" over her. Our nurse said it was very rare for the doctors to stay. These people were so good to us. The Lord used them to remind us of His presence in this intense darkness. (On August 22, 2010, exactly six months after her death, Dr. Lester sent me a recording of him singing that song, acapella, just like it would've been in her room. What a kind, kind man.)

We waited in that family room. I don't recall one word being spoken. Who knew what to say? The doctors came in together when it was over. It didn't take very long, and they said it was peaceful.

The three of us went in to see her one last time. No tubes. Total quiet. No machines beeping and sustaining life. It was the most deafening silence I've ever experienced. Peace? Not one bit. And it did not feel well with my soul.

David asked if he could cut a piece of her hair. Here was a husband desperate to take home anything he could from his wife. My heart ached with pain too deep for words, for David. We, of course, told him yes. He loved our daughter and wanted to hang on to anything of hers.

In that room, on that day, the space between Heaven and earth was thin. In that room, on that day, the presence of the Lord was thick.

***

David walked out of the room in front of us. I paused in the doorway. I put my hands on Rick's chest. Everything in me wanted to grab his shirt with both my hands but I made a conscious effort to just place them, palms down, on his chest, to stop him.

I looked Rick straight in the eyes with more desperation than there are words to tell you, "You have got to remind me that what we believe is truth."

What happened next is a firm memory, the fuel for my steps every day since this one. Stop whatever else you are doing right now and hear this, hear as though Rick were saying it straight to you:

"The tomb is empty."

Those words we have spoken over a million times since that day. They have been air to my soul when I couldn't find breath. They have been a drink of water when my heart was parched with burning grief. They have been the warm oil that poured into my open wounds as I ached with the very thought of living the rest of my days without our Jenny.

I had taught grief workshops for years, but I didn't know it felt quite like this. As a pastor's wife, I have sat with lots of grieving families. I didn't know it hurt like this.

"So, this is what it feels like. I didn't know it felt like this."

We walked through the long corridor toward the exit for the last time. This season began the fight for breath, the wrestle for hope, the groaning in prayer. All of these have now become a part of our lives. But walking through those corridors seemed like an ending and with every ending, there is a beginning. Everything in me totally rejected this new beginning.

The first task was for the three of us to tell a 9-year-old girl that her mommy was gone.

***

I don't want to forget the details of her death. That is hard to write because I still wish that her death was not part of my story. **But it is in the details of her death that I find Truths to cling to. Truths that will shore up my faith for the rest of my days walking on dirt.**

Where was hope? *Hope* had been cut right out of my heart. In place of that deep hole was a gaping open wound.

Who would've known it felt like this?

Chapter 3
Does God Like Funerals?
(Beverly)

The tomb is empty!

Everything in me clings to that truth.

Mike Cope, a well known preacher and a close family friend, says that we are living in the "not yet." We live in the days between Jesus' tomb being already empty and the promise that one day ours will be emptied too. But not yet. Just as the phrase *the tomb is empty* was becoming my anthem, we were preparing to put our Jenny in her tomb. The "not yet."

The Bible opens with a garden and a wedding, and it concludes with a garden and a wedding.
In the opening chapters of the first book in the Bible, Genesis, relationships were whole, healthy, and thriving. God was seen and heard, walking with His people. They were aware of His presence. In the beginning, people were hard-wired for life. Death was not a part of the beginning. Broken relationships were not in the beginning. Cancer was not in the beginning. Sepsis was not in the beginning.

But when the powers of darkness entered the story, those horrors became part of our common humanity. We have to learn to live with brokenness, while still clinging to our belief that God will restore it all one day.

One day there will be another garden and a wedding, the one mentioned at the end of Revelation. But for now, you and I walk the road in between the first garden and the forever garden. We walk the road between the first marriage, the one with Adam and Eve, and the forever marriage, the one with Jesus and His church. The one between Heaven and earth.

On the road in between the "already" and the "not yet," there is brokenness, pain, and suffering.

And, unfortunately, there are funerals.

Funerals. Is that what you call them? There is so much confusion around what to call them. A celebration of life? A memorial service? A farewell?

This isn't the only vocabulary struggle. We have a hard time finding a word for "death." We've attempted to take the harshness away by using softer words: *passing away*, *went to Heaven*, *went to see Jesus*, or *lost*. These can be confusing for children. We think children might be suicidal when they say they want to go to Heaven. No, they want to see their special person. I believe Jenny went to see the face of Jesus and is in Heaven, but I also needed to sit with the pain of her death ... and plan her funeral. And I just couldn't find a way to sweeten that up.

The visitation the night before the funeral was the first time I had been with people since Jenny's death. While we were in the hospital waiting room, I had found comfort in speaking words of encouragement and hope to the other hurting families. But now, I was void of words. There is such a deep awkward silence that death brings. So many people came to hug us and to remind us of the presence of God. I don't remember many of the individual moments, but together they fed my soul with love. It was a brief moment of total silence that stands out to me and continues to shape me.

Three friends from Abilene walked in: Randy Harris, Diane Cope, and Brady Bryce. I was standing close to Jenny's casket. When I saw these three, I had a question that bubbled to the top of a building geyser of confusion. Randy is a theologian, deep and thoughtful. Diane is a grieving mother after her daughter Megan's death in 1994 (at age 10). Brady had done grief work around his father's death.

When I saw these three, I couldn't keep the question in, "I can't picture Jenny happy in Heaven. How could she be happy without Malaya?"

Total silence.

Randy looked at the ground and shook his head softly.

Diane gazed into my eyes intently, as one who understands the pain.

Brady looked past me in the direction of Jenny's casket.

I closed my eyes to absorb this sacred moment. I knew I needed to explore the question in the silence of my own soul. Maybe I wasn't even asking the right question.

***

It just doesn't seem right to talk about Jenny's funeral without telling you a little about Jenny. It seems like a daunting task. I know most of you did not know Jenny. I'm guessing a lot of people at her funeral hadn't met her either. But they all felt like they knew her. People came from Memphis, Tennessee, where Josh continues to pastor; from Houston, Texas, where Jonathan was a worship pastor; and from Decatur, Texas, where Rick and I both have ministries. Some drove from San Antonio and towns in Oklahoma who didn't know anyone in our family, but they came because they had gotten caught up in the story. The Hills Church in North Richland Hills offered to let us use their building and they provided their livestream services for friends who couldn't attend in person. After praying over Jenny for 18 days, crowds of people felt connected to her although they had never met her face-to-face.

Jenny had a gift for walking with hurting hearts. Her best friend, Jessie, tells stories of Jenny ministering to her during her season with anxiety and depression. Jenny took Jessie to the grocery store with her, each pushing a cart. Jenny filled Jessie's cart with exactly what she was putting in her own. They cooked the exact same menus so Jenny could walk her through every step of meal prep. I love this! But my favorite story Jessie tells took place during a song of praise at their church, *The Met*. Jessie was seated with her head in her hands. Depression was deep. Jenny stood up for a song and with one gentle movement, took Jessie's hand, pulled her to her feet, and held Jessie's hand up in worship. It was such a sacred moment.

Jenny loved children. When she attended Abilene Christian University, they didn't offer a children's ministry degree yet, so she majored in Elementary Education and minored in Bible. She interned with a children's minister at an Abilene church to learn everything she could about teaching children about Jesus. For now, she settled on being a permanent substitute teacher at Malaya's school.

Jenny's love of children made it seem appropriate when the funeral director asked if we wanted to plan a funeral just for the children. He had never done anything like that before but felt like it was a really good time to try it. Of course, we wanted to provide any help we could for the children missing her already.

The children's pastors from The Met and The Hills, along with Jessie Beebe, planned the event. The children were given buttons with Jenny's picture and the word *Hope*, salvation bracelets, and a huge cake.

They gave the children permission to feel confused, sad, angry, and to remember Ms. Jenny with giggles. How could we not all laugh as we shared about Jenny's crazy dance moves, her love of *High School Musical*, and burping? Her dance moves might not win a competition, but her burping certainly could!

My favorite part of the children's funeral was an object lesson shared with me by a good friend during our planning. Since his dad died when he was a young child, he has helped many children and adults learn to walk through the mystery of death. Jessie did a beautiful job sharing his illustration.

She had a brownish flower in a brown clay pot.

Jessie said, "This pot represents Ms. Jenny's body and this flower represents her life before Ms. Jenny claimed Jesus as Lord. But when she called Jesus, "Lord," and was baptized, her life (her flower) was changed."

Jessie exchanged the brown flower for a beautiful, white flower, and said, "This is what happens to every one of us when we follow Jesus. Our yucky selves are exchanged for His beauty."

Joe, a friend, stood in front of this clay pot with his back to the crowd of listening children. With one swift, skillful move, he broke that clay pot into pieces.

"That," Jessie said, "is what happened to Jenny's body on Monday. Her body was broken, and Ms. Jenny died."

Jessie took the flower that represents Jenny's life in Jesus and placed it into a beautiful crystal vase. It was stunning and every child was riveted.

"This is Ms. Jenny now! She has been given a new, glorious body!"

And with that Jessie opened the good news of Jesus to these young ears.

A beautiful slideshow of Jenny's life started to the music of *I Can Only Imagine*. Rick and I were standing in the back of the room. When that song started, I was overwhelmed by raw emotion. I turned to lean against the brick wall, face first. My cheek felt the brick and I made this weird move with my hand like I was trying to grab the brick. It was hard and unmoving. I couldn't find anything to hold on to, to cling to, to steady myself with, because I was up against a brick wall. I carried that feeling into the adult funeral which immediately followed.

At the conclusion, the children walked outside and released balloons to their friend, Ms. Jenny. Malaya released one to her mommy.

Then, we went into the large sanctuary, overflowing with people, where Jonathan opened his sister's funeral with this story:

Although Jenny and David got pregnant with Malaya easily, Jenny struggled with secondary infertility. She and David had done everything to have another baby. By everything, I mean those horrible pills that can make you cry for hours, surgery, and treatments that cost the price of a small car. Jenny had always dreamed of having a full house of children to teach and train up to follow Jesus. Jenny loved being Malaya's mom. Malaya filled her heart with purpose, and she wanted more purpose.

Month after month there had been such sadness and disappointment. Jenny was fearful the cloud of depression was setting in over her. Our family decided we would all fast from something every single day to remind us to pray over Jenny's heart and her womb. She and David didn't know about our commitment. At Thanksgiving that year, Jenny called a family meeting. After a fabulous meal, she began to read some verses to us about hope. I have poured through her Bible, but I can't remember what verses she read.

But I remember this. Jenny said, "Mom, do you remember when I was a little girl and you taught me to plan my funeral?"

I did remember that. I taught my children to pick out two or three characteristics that they wanted to be remembered for, words they wanted spoken at their funerals, and to live their lives centering on those values. It just never occurred to me that I would be present at one of their funerals.

Jenny said, "I don't want people to walk by my casket someday and say, 'Oh there's that poor infertile woman.' I want people to walk by my casket and say, 'There is a woman who continued to praise and serve the Lord when she didn't get her way.'"

"Today, that is our family," Jonathan said. "We didn't get our way, but we will not stop praising and serving the Lord. And we are inviting you to join us."

Jonathan was anointed. How do you sing in front of hundreds of people on the saddest day of your life? You do it when the Lord anoints you to do it. We sang the songs that I know we will sing in Heaven around the throne: *Blessed Be Your Name, Worthy is the Lamb, Mighty to Save, The Revelation Song,* and *In Christ Alone.* We declared His victory over death while feeling so defeated by death.

I'm not sure how to describe what happened as we all stood and praised the One we choose to follow. The words of every song were so familiar, but every word was taking on new depth. Through most every song, I was standing with my hands lifted toward the Heavens, like a little girl reaching out to be held in her daddy's arms. I wanted Him to rescue us from this pain.

Rick and I were sitting with Malaya and David. When Malaya was standing, I was standing. When Malaya was overwhelmed with emotion and seated, I sat to hold her. I wanted Him to rescue Malaya. I honestly didn't know what to do. I wanted Jenny back. She would know.

Josh, also anointed by the Spirit, moved to the podium to bring words of Hope and encouragement. He paused. He prayed. He said what we all knew - that a 26-year-old and a 29-year-old should not be on a stage presiding over the funeral of their 31-year-old sister.

After the prayer, Josh went for humor, "Our family hasn't cried this much since *Fresh Prince* went off the air in 1996. Our family used to reenact scenes from this show. I was Will, Jenny was Hillary, Dad was Uncle Phil, and Jonathan was Carlton." Laughter was perfect in that moment. It was so human and so sacred.

He told some funny stories about Jenny. Jenny loved her family and was a fierce warrior to protect all of us. She could come across as quiet, introverted, more reserved. But when she felt that one of *her people* were being wronged, there was a fierceness about her that could scare grown men.

Here is a story Josh shared at her funeral and in his first book, *Scarred Faith*:

When I was a freshman in high school, I asked a girl if she wanted to go to the movies with me. Like it is for most freshmen, a date to the movies meant that Mom has to drop off a minivan full of ninth graders who are embarrassed to ride in a minivan. I don't even remember what movie we saw, but I remember that this girl had been on my radar and I was just thrilled to be at a movie with her. I wasted no time putting my arm around her, and before the movie was over we had enjoyed the thrill of making out in a movie theater. (Give me some grace. I was in ninth grade.)

Later that night I called the girl to chat - that was before Facebook and text messaging - and a guy answered the phone - and let's just say he wasn't very happy. Little did I know that I was kissing a girl who was dating a senior from another school. This guy proceeded to tell me that if I ever called her again he was going to get his boys, come to my house, and kill me - literally. I heard someone pick up a phone on the other side of my house. It was my protective older sister, Jenny. She yelled, "Listen here, you little *******! If you ever call over here again threatening my brother, I'm going to jump through this phone and kick your little ***!" He hung up. These were probably two of the five curse words Jenny said her entire life. A moment later, she rounded the corner with her fists in the air like she had come to save the day. Half of me wanted to jump up and congratulate her for her bravery. The other half of me felt deflated, because what would my friends say when they found out my sister was fighting my battles for me?[5]

Wait? What? Jenny cussed? Laughter. Reminding us of our humanity.

He spoke over each of us and focused on the treasured relationship we each share with Jenny.

"David, you were a brother before you were a brother-in-law. We couldn't have asked for a man to come into Jenny's life to love her the way you did. We are in this together for life."

"Malaya, we are going to fight for your faith. We are going to fight for you to know Jesus."

"Mom, your daughter became your best friend. She adored you."

"Dad, you called her your princess. You and Mom raised us to love Jesus. You pointed us to Him. And we are going to cling to Him today and forever."

He called Jonathan onto the stage, and they knelt together in prayer, asking us to join their kneeling posture. We declared that the power of darkness would not have the last word. We declared that Jesus wins. Our voices may have been a bit shaky, but we spoke what we were desperate to own. *The tomb is empty.*

Then it was Jonathan's turn at the brotherly banter. "There was one time our family cried harder than when *Fresh Prince* went off the air; when *Saved by the Bell* went off. I was Zach. Jenny was Kelly. And you were Screech. And Mom, I want you to know that I never made out in a movie theater." I treasure those moments of laughter.

---

[5] Josh Ross, *Scarred Faith*, (New York: Howard Books, 2013), 24.

Jonathan introduced a recording of Jenny singing "How Beautiful." Jenny and Jonathan had sung it as a duet for Jonathan's wife, Jennifer, to walk down the aisle at their wedding. The joy on Jenny's face after she spent time in the recording studio will forever be imprinted on my heart. She was overwhelmed with gratitude to get to record this with her brother!

Rick Atchley concluded Jenny's funeral by speaking a word for Jesus. He shared from John 11 about Lazarus' death. He focused on Jesus's words to Lazarus's sisters in verse 40, "Did I not tell you that if you believe, you will see the glory of God?"

A grieving sibling's heart-cry: "Where were You, Lord?"

Jesus' announcement that He is the resurrection and the life.

Jesus' raw compassion at his friends' pain and suffering.

The acknowledgment that Jesus could have prevented it.

And that even in pain, the glory of God can be revealed. Maybe, mostly when in pain, the glory of God can be revealed.

The glory of God was revealed through our sons that day.

The glory of God was revealed through our precious daughters-in-law walking with our family while taking care of very young children and ministering to their broken-hearted husbands.

The glory of God was revealed through David, who was trying to comfort a 9-year-old little girl.

The glory of God was revealed through Malaya who was trying to absorb the impossible.

The glory of God was revealed through a huge crowd of family and friends who gathered to support us as we were learning to carry this heavy weight of suffering.

***

What was the rest of life going to look like without Jenny? Dr. Kollipara, Dr. Lester, and our nurses had been there to walk us through our time in the hospital. The funeral home had walked us through the next few days. But now …

Who can tell you what to do when no one knows what to do?

***

Two weeks after Jenny's death, I called Dr. Kollipara's office to see if David, Rick, and I could meet with him. We had so many questions. His receptionist was kind but told me that he didn't do that. But she did take my number. Within thirty seconds my phone rang. It was Dr. Kollipara. He agreed to meet with us and to have Dr. Lester there too.

We sat in the same room where they had told us that it was over. When the doctors walked in, they directed their attention straight toward David. "It was not your fault. What happened to Jenny couldn't have been predicted. We are trained professionals and it could've happened to us." Compassion flowed. They answered our questions so gently. As far as we have come in the treatment of infectious diseases, there is still so much that is unknown.

***

Doing the most normal things felt impossible.

I would walk into Walmart and do a u-turn right out the door. What I wanted to do was scream, "How are you people still shopping? Do you not know Jenny died?"

I saw three grief therapists to make sure I was mourning in a healthy way. When you are a counselor, you are in counseling often, just usually over chips and salsa, or breadsticks.

One of my grief counselors said this to me, "Strength is way overrated. Give it up." From her I learned to give up trying to be strong, replacing that with a desire to be brave.

Another told me that I needed to pray to become *content in this mystery*. From him I learned that *why* isn't the best question. There wasn't an answer to satisfy my soul.

And the third one told me that I was being an overachiever at grief. From him I learned to trust the process of grief. Grief is not to be conquered or managed, but rather carried.

***

In the middle of the night about two weeks after Jenny's death, I couldn't sleep and I went to the bathroom, laid on the rug, and cried out to the Lord, "Where are You, Lord? Do you see me? Do you hear me?"

Immediately my phone began to light up. (I carried it with me in case David needed help in the night.) Three friends texted me. One lived in another state. One was an acquaintance from the other side of the world. One was a close friend. They each texted me something like: "We wanted you to have this message when you woke up. The Lord is near."

I pictured Jesus gently moving my hair out of my face as He lay beside me. He saw me. He heard me.

***

On our first trip to Israel, when we got to the traditional site of Jesus' tomb, I asked our guide if this was really "it." What did it mean to be the traditional site? Our guide was an Arabic Christian and a revered teacher, very well respected among the Israeli people. He had this way of rocking from heel to toe when he was teaching. He stared at the ground, rocking, and answered me, "We don't know if this is the exact site, because He wasn't there long enough." I absolutely love that!

Until the day comes when the tombs are emptied, we will continue to gather at graves on Easter Sunday and remember that we are expecting them to be opened … one day. When the way gets hard, we whisper in each other's ears or we shout into the largest of gatherings, "*The tomb is empty!*" And with that, we will find the courage to get up again. And with that, God keeps showing up for funerals.

Chapter 4
The Birth of Hope
(Beverly)

"Her absence is like the sky, spread over everything."
- C.S. Lewis, *A Grief Observed*[6]

In December 2009, Jenny, Malaya, and I walked into one of our favorite stores to do some last-minute Christmas shopping. We parked quite a distance from the entrance, so Malaya and I had plenty of time to sing and dance our way to the door. While grabbing a cart, I saw Jenny head for the restroom. Her speed made me think she was sick, so I followed her. When I rounded the corner, I heard her sobbing.

"Jenny?"

"Mom, did you see them? Everyone we passed was either pregnant or had a newborn."

Nope, I hadn't noticed. **When your heart is yearning for something so deeply that there is an intense, unrelenting ache, it can appear that every other person has what you are desperate to get.**

I've heard it from my friends and clients for years:
- When half of your couple is *missing* or if you aren't part of a twosome, you can feel so out of place and lonely at dinner parties and at church, surrounded by seemingly happy couples.
- When you are struggling financially, your friends are taking exotic vacations or buying the latest super cool gadgets.
- When your marriage is in trouble, you notice other couples holding hands and exchanging connecting glances over inside jokes.
- When your health is struggling, everyone else seems to be a runner.
- When your daughter has died, every day seems to be "your daughter is a vital part of your life" day.

After Jenny's death, my pain was not only missing my daughter, but missing Malaya's mommy. I fell in love with my first-born grandchild before I had ever seen her face or heard her newborn cries. With her birth, there was part of me that breathed its first breath, too. Grandparenting is very different from parenting. As a Grammy, we could

---
[6] C.S. Lewis, *A grief observed* (New York: HarperCollins, 1961), 11.

have ice cream or snow cones for appetizers. We could sing out loud and dance through department stores. It's not because I couldn't do those things before, but I didn't give myself permission to do them before there was this grandchild.

I was gripped with a deep ache for what Malaya's future held without Jenny. Grief is always hard, but watching children grieve ups the ante by millions. During my tenure as a first-grade teacher, I had a student who watched his younger brother die in the summer before first grade. Landon was mute when school started. He lost his words with the death of his brother. His mom felt so helpless, believing she lost both her children with the death of one.

There had to be a way to hold space with grieving children, and I knew I had to find it. I refused to stand by and watch my granddaughter suffer without offering the best tools available. I read books on children's grief, attended workshops, and made phone calls to experts. The best advice came from others who knew this story as part of their own.

When a tragedy happens, we can experience a disconnect from *normal* society. This disconnect can be either real or perceived. We are forced to join another club. One we never would have chosen. The members of this club would do anything to get out, but there is no exit. A sacred connection forms between hearts that grieve. I found myself asking fellow club members about growing up without a parent.

Do you remember your special person?

What traditions do you keep alive?

Do you hang the Christmas stocking?

***

I am the Founder and Executive Director of a non-profit counseling center, Wise County Christian Counseling (WCCC). I had been a stay-at-home mom for twelve years, learning to love and protect my own three children. I had been a first-grade teacher for twelve years, offering that love and protection to the children placed in my classroom. In 2010, I had been a licensed professional counselor for eight years, teaching mommies and daddies how to create homes that offer love and protection to the next generation. All my counseling work continues to be done within the framework of a nonprofit, where professional services are offered on a sliding scale. Emotional pain does not know economic boundaries, and my desire was to offer professional counseling to all people.

But now? Would anyone want to come to a grieving mother for help? Even if they did come, would I, a woman with a crushed heart, be able to help? It took months for me to get back into the counseling room. My own anxiety would not allow me to hold space with other hurting humans without a tsunami of tears flowing from my own raw wound.

The story of the growth of WCCC can only be told from hindsight. When I was living it, the changes were so subtle, each new movement inching in slowly and with intense certainty, not requiring much time to think or process, but requiring acceptance. While I was fearful that my life in ministry was closing, the Lord was beginning to build it.

The day before Jenny went into the hospital, Miriam Cowles joined my team of one. I'm not sure what would've happened to WCCC had Miriam not been there to keep it afloat during this season. A few months later, a play therapist knocked on my office door asking for a job. There were more knocks, more counselors, eventually creating an amazing team of fourteen counselors. I want to be clear; my only role was keeping the eyes and hands of my heart open to what the Lord was doing. I prayed over and over, "Lord, please help me not to miss what You are doing in my life. Help me to keep my eyes on You and my hands open to Your gifts."

He kept focusing my heart's eye on children -- from my own, to my classroom, and now to my grandchildren. I am obsessed with equipping the next generation, giving the best tools possible to walk out hard paths. In November 2017, I hosted a brunch for women on staff at churches in our community. We discussed ways we could assist them in their dreams for the future. You can imagine how my ears perked up when one of the children's pastors turned to her friend and said, "We need a grief center for children." Why, yes we do. That is exactly what we need. I knew we needed a safe place where children could discuss their grief in age appropriate groups. Malaya was now seventeen, but how I wish she had a place like the one we were going to create.

I am not a fan of statistics. We can get lost in the numbers and forget the faces and the real-life stories. But statistics can be helpful in developing a big picture view. There is a wonderful grief center in Denver, *Judi's House*, that also serves as a research center. They found that in the United States, one of every sixteen children will either have a parent or a sibling die. This statistic does not include grandparents or other extended family. Those numbers are staggering to me. That means there might be a grieving child in every classroom. But so many of these children stay silent about the pain for fear of being *different* and living doused with sympathy and pity.

People, children included, can't thrive under the umbrella of sympathy and pity. Sympathy and pity create a chasm between the wounded and the ones not yet wounded. Empathy is the human emotion that is exhibited alongside a hurting heart, showing up to help carry the pain. We all need safe places to tell our stories, unfolding them without pressure or rushing. And that was my dream for a grief center. To provide creative ways to remember our special people, and empathic space to learn how to carry the pain of their deaths.

I could hardly wait until our next board meeting to discuss this idea of adding a new component to WCCC. Unanimously, the board approved! In March 2017, at our annual fundraiser, I stood on a stage in front of several hundred people and announced our dream of opening a grief center for children, teens, and adults. This dream had a name: *Jenny's Hope*.

Applause broke out. I stood there for a split-second absorbing what I had spoken aloud in front of this crowd who would now hold me accountable. As I walked off the stage, I paused behind a column before heading to the back to shake hands. "Oh Lord, what did I just do? I don't know how to do this." The Lord responded, "Watch Me."

"I don't know how to do this." How many times had I uttered that phrase since February 2010? "I don't know how to do this, but all I know to do is to stay behind You, Lord. I want to be so close to You that the dust from Your steps gets in my own shoes."

There was never a question what I wanted the name of our grief center to be. Jenny had taught me so much about hope as she clung to the hope of having another baby. I had watched her *hope* evolve with time into something deeply spiritual. *Jenny's Hope* was rooted in the name of Jesus, Jenny's Jesus.

***

People frequently say to me, "The Lord really answers your prayers." To which I respond, "I don't have a clue how to pray this stuff. I ask Him for more of Him." If I have to walk this road, Lord, please show me how to do it in a way that brings You honor and glory. I don't believe that God is the cause of pain, but I firmly believe that He doesn't waste a second of it. He can use the mess we give Him to make a beautiful picture. He can bring meaning from our confusion.

In a podcast with Brené Brown, David Kessler discusses his most recent book, *Finding Meaning: The Sixth Stage of Grief.* Dr. Kessler says that meaning is not found *in* the death but in what we do *after* the death. However, he cautions against rushing into the meaning to avoid the pain. "We cannot heal what we do not allow ourselves to feel," he says.[7]

For the last seven years, I had given myself permission to feel sadness, confusion, and even joy. I had watched the Lord grow a counseling center around me. He grew me as a leader while He drew counselors to join in this ministry. It is now *our* ministry. And our ministry was ready to open a new dimension, groups for grieving children. Malaya's face was always in the forefront of my mind as I prepared.

***

There were two barriers that I knew the Lord would have to show me how to jump over.
1. I didn't know the first step about creating a grief center. All I had in my mind's eye was the finished product. We have all seen lots of dreams die with lack of the first step.
2. We didn't have the physical space to open a grief center. Our creative counselors even made closets into offices and play rooms. We didn't have any extra rooms for another component to our existing ministry.

Through a lot of networking, the Lord introduced me to the National Alliance for Grieving Children. This is a wonderful group of people who, collectively, offer a variety of first steps. I attended their conference in North Carolina gathering support, curriculums, enthusiasm, and a full awareness that I couldn't do this by myself.

The Lord brought to us an award-winning teacher. Devon had decided to get a Master's in Counseling, and she agreed to be the Coordinator for *Jenny's Hope*. She has a heart for hurting children, for writing lesson plans, and for organizing volunteers. We have formed a sacred partnership.

However, at the time, we still needed a space. My board members and I looked at lots of buildings. None worked out. One owner wanted way more than we could afford. One owner didn't call me back. One was an old house with no insulation between rooms - not soundproof enough to host groups. There had to be something that we could make work, but nothing appeared available.

Until …

---

[7] Brené Brown, *Unlocking Us* (podcast), David Kessler and Brené on Grief and Finding Meaning, March 31, 2020, https://brenebrown.com/podcast/david-kessler-and-brene-on-grief-and-finding-meaning/.

Pam Wood, one of my prayer warriors, had been driving all over town praying for a location for us. Thanksgiving morning, in 2017, she texted me, "The Lord told me where the grief center is supposed to be." Those words made my heart jump, but not in a good way. Surely, like me, you've had somebody tell you the Lord told them that you were supposed to teach the two-year-old class for the rest of your life. Those words are somehow considered like an ace card. Who can argue with the Lord? But I loved time with Pam, and I was curious, so we set up a coffee date the following week.

Pam and her family owned *The Gift Shop*. We had met years earlier while I was shopping for Webkinz to add to Malaya's collection when she was a little girl. (I've always loved helping Malaya collect things!) There was an instantaneous connection between us, but Pam connects well with all people. Pam's brother-in-law, Josh Wood, died in December 2010, the same year as Jenny. Our hearts connected even more deeply through our grief journeys. Pam had decided to close *The Gift Shop* in July 2017, the same year I began looking for space for a grief center. The Lord connected our lives, and our stories, for His glory, for His beauty from our ashes.

When we met at our favorite coffee shop, I started chatting quickly. Pam excitedly said she couldn't wait for one more second to tell me that the Lord told her we were supposed to open the grief center in (drumroll, please) *The Gift Shop*, a beautiful storefront located in a well-trafficked area! Whoa! I totally agreed with Pam and with the Lord. *The Gift Shop* was more than a dream -- it was simply gorgeous. Situated under a clock tower with a beautiful fountain, the building holds inside a granite laid staircase with custom carpet, a cozy fireplace, and a kitchen. The beauty of this place totally supersedes my words on this page.

So, with the Wood family's full permission, the remodel of *The Gift Shop* started. We had almost 7,000 square feet of open space. The first time the project coordinator and I met, his first question was "What do you envision here?" I said, "I picture something warm, inviting, sacred space." He responded with kindness, "I'm talking about the walls. Where do you want the walls?" "Well, that's not my gift. I have no clue. Just whatever you think." Thank you, my friend, for not laughing out loud! I had spoken the truth. I had no clue how to form the rooms, but I was watching all of them come together and rise up around me. I was watching it. God was making it.

There were many walls to add and there was only one wall coming down. I met the crew early on February 26, 2018, exactly eight years and a day after Jenny's funeral. I put on a hard hat and swung a sledge hammer as I quoted Isaiah 61:

The Spirit of the Sovereign Lord is on me, because the LORD has anointed me to proclaim good news to the poor. He has sent me to bind up the brokenhearted, to proclaim freedom for the captives and release from darkness for the prisoners, to proclaim the year of the Lord's favor ... to comfort all who mourn, and provide for those who grieve...To bestow on them a crown of beauty instead of ashes, the oil of joy instead of mourning, and a garment of praise instead of spirit of despair. They will be called oaks of righteousness, a planting of the Lord for the display of His splendor.[8]

And with that reading, the wall was down, and rebuilding began. The sacred space of *The Gift Shop* became the sacred space of Jenny's Hope. I would go up early in the morning and late at night and walk the forming hallways, praying for healing in my own heart, in our family, and in whoever else would join us in this journey.

***

We knew we needed a logo. I immediately knew what I wanted. In his book, *A Grace Disguised*, Jerry Sittser, says that when his grief was overwhelming, he felt like he was staring at the stump of a huge tree that had just been cut down in his backyard.

"That stump, which sat all alone, kept reminding me of the beloved tree that I had lost. ... Eventually, however, I decided to do something about it. I landscaped my backyard, reclaiming it once again as my own. I decided to keep the stump there, since it was both too big and too precious to remove. Instead of getting rid of it, I worked around it. I planted shrubs, trees, flowers, and grass. The stump remains but is surrounded by a blooming garden of beautiful flowers. The sorrow remains, but that what was once ugly is now an integral part of a larger, lovely whole."[9]

I knew the logo for *Jenny's Hope* had to have daffodils. Daffodils bloom in February. They are the Flower of Hope. So, we chose a stump surrounded by daffodils. We had it engraved in stone.

On August 3, 2018, Jenny's 40th birthday, I received an early morning text from a friend who had driven past our offices and saw the sign for our grief center going up. I texted the project manager immediately. Did he somehow know? Did he know it was Jenny's birthday? He did not.

He had no clue. But the Giver of the best gifts knew. So, with a wink and a nod from Him, *Jenny's Hope* was ready to open its doors.

---

[8] Isaiah 61:1-3.
[9] Jerry Sittser, *A Grace Disguised*, (Grand Rapids: Zondervan, 2004), 51.

Finally, it was time to host our first session of *Jenny's Hope*. Grieving families came. They listened. They responded. It was such a deep blessing to watch their faces soften a little more each week. We were learning together. We were sharing our stories, our hearts, and our journeys. With each of their faces, I saw Malaya's face, her eyes.

***

With the dream of *Jenny's Hope* becoming a reality, my own journey took a strange turn. A suspicious spot appeared during a routine mammogram. My family history does not include cancer. I had walked through suspicious spots before. I followed up with an ultrasound and a biopsy. I was determined not to let this distract me from the joy of the birth of *Jenny's Hope*. I couldn't help but be a little ticked at my body. I needed every bit of physical and emotional energy to accomplish what my spirit was desperate to do - to be with and support grieving families.

Some things don't care if you are ticked or not, if you choose them or not, if the timing is good or not (seriously, is it ever?). Three weeks into our eight-week sessions of *Jenny's Hope*, I got the call that I had invasive and noninvasive breast cancer. I was at Main Event with two grandchildren and their friends, and with Kim, David's new wife, and her boys when the doctor called me. The doctor could hear the background noise and asked me if I would rather she call back. No. I would head for the exit. I didn't want a call back. I wanted to know now. I wanted it to be over before it even started. Tell me what I have. Tell me the plan to fix it. Tell me when we can start the process so I can get back to *Jenny's Hope*.

I stood on that sidewalk, hearing her words, too dumbfounded to ask any questions, wondering how on earth I was going to tell Rick, my kids, and my grandchildren. No, I don't want to tell them. I didn't want my body to be the source of their fear. It was interesting the way the Lord nudged my closest circle to call me. I walked back into Main Event and told Kim. We looked at each other without saying much. My daughter-in-law, Jenn, called to check on her kids. I told her - cancer. She offered to meet me immediately, but I assured her I was ok. I needed to tell Rick. So, I called him, a call that was full of unspoken questions. Then my phone rang, and Josh was calling from his family vacation in Florida to check in. I told him and felt the heavy sadness across the phone line. Each call seemed so ordained. But my grandchildren.

I didn't want to tell my grandchildren, but I knew those were necessary conversations. We had to walk this together. I am a proponent of speaking age-appropriate truth to children. They needed to hear it from me. They needed to hear a plan from me. The physical plan would be up to the doctors. But our family's spiritual plan needed to come from me. I had just completed filming a Bible study on YouTube called "Clinging to Hope." I teach that we don't cling to the hope of what we want, but to the Hope of His presence invading our very own hearts. I wanted to tell my grandchildren how we were going to walk this out with faith.

I called Malaya first. I didn't want her to wonder if she could trust me to tell the truth. She was a freshman in college, and I knew she had tremendous adult support.

Josh, Kayci, and their boys FaceTimed me that night. Everyone had questions, and I had few answers. Our youngest grandchild asked a profound question: "Are you going to die?" Well, isn't that what we all want to know? Am I going to die? "I am going to die, but not from this."

When I told Jonathan and Jennifer's kids, their eyes never left mine. "I've got something to tell you. Before I tell you what has happened, I want to tell you that, as of right now, the doctor is calling it the best case scenario."

Since Jenny's death, I had grown accustomed to my presence creating pain. It had become a stark reminder that we don't always get our way, that people really do die. I had gathered a group of broken-hearted parents, guardians, and children. Oh Lord, the children. Had we gathered these children for them to have a front-row view to another battle for life, my battle for my own life. *Please, Father, help me not to be another story of fear for them.*

A month after my surgery to remove the cancer, I was ready to begin radiation. I had a wonderful radiation tech. When we met, we exchanged our stories. I told her about Jenny, and she told me that her only sibling, her brother, died the day before Jenny went into the hospital. As she was sliding me into the CT machine, I asked her how she was. She began to cry and was still crying as she said, "You are the first person to ever ask me that."

"I'm the first person to ask you how you are?"

"Yes, everyone else asks me how my parents are doing."

Sibling loss is the least written about; the least addressed. So, my new friend and I spent every radiation treatment with her talking about her grief and teaching me how to hold space with the siblings.

Thank you, Lord, for using my treatments to teach me what I need to know to help the children at *Jenny's Hope*.

***

We open and close every night of *Jenny's Hope* with Bill Withers' song, "Lean on Me." We ask the children to decide in advance who they want to *lean on*. The first night they choose their parent or guardian. After that it often expands to include a facilitator in their group. Sometimes it has even been another child that they know understands the path.

Isn't that a life skill? We have to know who our people are, the ones that when we can lean on when the way gets hard. It is always sacred space to bear witness to the movement that takes place over the eight weeks of *Jenny's Hope*. The smiles, the laughter, the shared stories, the common tears, and the Light of Hope for the journey.

We end every night, just like I end every meeting and session, by quoting together Romans 15:13. It was Jenny's life verse. Now it's mine.

> *"May the God of Hope fill you with all joy and peace as you trust in Him, so that you may overflow with Hope by the power of the Holy Spirit."*

***

Recently, our event-planning team was meeting to discuss some future events. They were listening to me share again the details of the birth of *Jenny's Hope*. Tears were flowing for all of us as I recounted my own beauty-*from*-ashes story. The *from* in that phrase seems like such a little word. No meaning really. But don't let it fool you. That *from* is loaded with some of the hardest work I have ever done. One of my close friends calls what happens in that *from* - "blessable posture."

From the earliest of days, I begged the Lord, sometimes through only groanings, to open the eyes and the hands of my heart to Him, to what He was doing. I wanted the Lord to use my pain. If I have to hurt this deeply, please don't let it be for nothing.

Maybe for you it's a broken relationship, chronic pain, rejection, isolation, or addiction. Listen to me, the Lord does not waste a moment of your pain. Whatever we hold loosely and give to Him, He will use.

It is discipline. It is a decision. It is hard. It is worth it. It can feel unsettling to wait in *blessable posture*. But when we do, we bear witness to a story bigger than our own. The Lord is sewing together His masterpiece and using our stories as part of His own.

Jenny's Hope was birthed through *blessable posture*.

Jenny did not die so Wise County could open its first grief center, but *since* Jenny died, Wise County can open its first grief center. This is not the story I would've chosen but this is the story I have. May the Lord give me a Scarred Hope that encourages and blesses others as we walk together, side-by-side, and arm-in-arm.

<u>Introduction to Section 2</u>
(Beverly)

Some good family friends came over to visit when I was about four-years-old. My mom had sent me to take a quick bath before their arrival. Those two words still don't go together. There is nothing quick about a bath. Connie, a 12-year-old, peeked around the corner of the bathroom to surprise me. When I saw her, I began to splash wildly and yell, "Get me out!" Connie grabbed the nearest towel and stood me up on the potty where I began to dance wildly. In one grand gesture of '60s-style dancing, I slid right off that potty, busting my chin. I have never danced on a potty again -- ever. A scar on my chin also reminds me that it is a really bad idea.

Maybe you have a scar of something silly that you did or an accident that you recovered from. Or maybe you have a scar from something that wasn't your fault at all. Sometimes things just happen, leaving a scar that has formed over a deep-set wound.

Jenny's death left a different kind of wound, and one I wasn't sure would ever form a scar. My heart was crushed. How does one put a heart back together?

***

When I was a first-grade teacher, I always taught a unit on the State of Alaska. One of the animals native to Alaska is the musk ox. When musk ox sense a predator is near, they circle around their babies and their wounded, staring at the attacking beast as if to say, "You can't have them." There are other animals who do this, but none looks uglier than the musk ox.

I've spent a lot of days in my life like the big mama musk ox protecting those younger and those wounded. I've looked different perceived enemies in the eye, declaring, "Not today. You will have to get through me first."

In 2010, it was my turn in the middle. I was so wounded, and the enemy seemed to be pressing in hard to devour my faith and my testimony. Many friends rose up to encircle me and my family and face off with the enemy saying, "You can't have her. You won't be able to get to them without going through me first." They let me lay in the middle and learn to walk again. My legs were wobbly and unstable. But the protection was thick and fierce.

Now, I'm in and out of that circle, but for the most part, I'm on the outside looking for those in need of protection. It was never an accident moving from the inside, lying on the ground, gasping for breath, and to the outside again. Every move was with intentional direction and energy.

In Part 1, we shared the details that put us in the middle of that circle. In Part 2, we share the disciplines we practice to stand back up and to move back out. The strategies in Part 2 have been used by hundreds of wounded hearts and they have proved effective. As you read through Part 2, be ready to stand a little straighter, and to roar a little louder.

Chapter 5

Grief as a Gift
(Beverly)

I love words. I use a lot of them. In fact, when I was six, I was super excited to start school because it seemed like the easiest way to make a whole bunch of brand new friends. The first day of first grade was a success. I made LOTS of friends, including Donna Ohlund, who would be my bestie for the next twelve years. On the second day of first grade, I fast-walked into my classroom at Lamar Elementary in La Marque, Texas, where I grew up. Fast-walk is what rule-following students do when running is forbidden. I was so excited to see Donna and all of my other new friends. But when I excitedly slid around the corner heading into my classroom, I couldn't find my desk anywhere. I did find my teacher, Mrs. Landers, to inquire about its absence.

Apparently, she was expecting my question because her finger was already pointing to a desk all alone by the windows. "You talked all day yesterday, Bevie, so today you'll have to sit over there. School is for learning." My excited little eyes followed her long pointy finger. I knew immediately that Mrs. Landers was determined to make my social life a challenge.

I am proud to tell you that Mrs. Landers became a Christian years later.

I'm also proud to tell you that school didn't get in the way of my abundance of words. Ever.

Words.

The words in Jesus' parable in Luke 6:46-49 hold some beautiful truths. Grab a pen right now and underline the following words in your Bibles: "As for everyone who hears my words and **puts them into practice**, I will show you what they are like. They are like a man building a house, who **dug down deep...**"

Swim with me as we head into deeper waters. Let's discuss some words and their definitions that can either fuel our faith or kill it. These words were a part of my vocabulary before Jenny's death, but since then, they have taken on deeper meanings. They convict, heal, penetrate, and give me something to cling to. These words also can be misused. These words, while frequently used in religious cliques, can suffocate the air right out of our wandering, wondering hearts. But there is life-breath to be found in their depth. They are concepts to be **put into practice** by **digging down deep.**

Get a gulp of air, hold your nose (or whatever you do when you go underwater), and let's dive in!

Trust

Trust is an essential component in connected relationships. Broken trust is frequently the catalyst for setting an appointment with me, a counselor. We don't have to be very old in life before we discover that trust can be risky business. People can break your trust without intention. Some of us even break trust with ourselves. But what happens when trusting God comes into question? Please, somebody, tell me I'm not the only one! When the voice of fear gets loud, the voice of trust can grow really quiet. Our ears strain to hear it.

While Rick was on sabbatical last summer, we spent a few days at a friend's remote hunting cabin. On our last night at the cabin, we decided to take one last walk through the pasture. The weeds were high and the insects were hopping. It was a path that had become familiar, so we knew when to jump over on the right side of the path because of an upcoming hole in the road and when to stay on the left. We knew the markers to gauge the time we had left before dark, if we stayed on this familiar path.

Everything was so calm and relaxing until Rick caught sight of a new path that he really wanted to try. It is hard for me to walk away from a new adventure, so we quickly decided to try it out. At first it was an easier path. We followed a fence and saw lots of deer blinds.

All of a sudden, the new path got steeper. There were more rocks, higher weeds, and it was getting darker. The sun was going down and we were on an unfamiliar path, and it was getting harder to walk. The coyotes were beginning to howl. Did I mention we had on shorts and tennis shoes?

I was right behind Rick, trying to match his steps so we could watch for snakes. Rick said the only thing that could be dangerous for us would be a wild mama hog with babies. He said the coyotes would stay away from us, and I wanted to believe that to be true. I was trying to look down for snakes, and look up for hogs and coyotes.

I had my phone with me, but it didn't have a full charge. We might need that flashlight. I checked in with Rick to see how much charge he had on his phone. He had left it at the cabin. Lovely! It is getting darker. The coyotes are getting louder. Rick loves the sound of howling coyotes. I don't. Those howls are creepy. It sounds like they are gathering, starving, and drooling.

My mind raced. *Good Morning America* had been running stories about people surviving in the wilderness. Well, mostly surviving. Not everyone in their stories survived. And we had just watched the new *Lion King* where the coyotes and the hyenas circled their victims. *GMA* and *Lion King* scenes were joining into one script in my head. I started to express my frustration -- well that's a nice way to put what I was expressing. It sounded more like whining with an edge.

Rick stopped, turned to look at me, all so quickly since it was almost dark, and said firmly, "Trust me." And I did. I had to decide all over again, after almost 43 years of marriage, that I was going to trust him. At this point, he was the best option, really the only option. I have followed him before on some pretty treacherous paths and he has always found the way out.

When the new path became impossible, we turned around, arriving back to the cabin just as the darkness settled over us. We had to turn on the porch light to pull the burrs from our socks. But we made it. There was a definite "chi-ching" in the trust bucket. My man led me to safety, again!

Trust is not always easy, and it is never a gift, but it can be earned through trustworthy behavior. It's like there is a bridge between your heart and another person's heart. When you first meet, you go shopping for wood together. Some bridges are made out of really great wood. Others are made out of thin wood or wood with lots of holes. Sometimes our bridges get blown up and we have to decide if we want to start all over by shopping for wood again to rebuild that bridge.

From a spiritual perspective, the Lord has invited us to walk a bridge formed between His heart and ours.

***

From the earliest days of Jenny's diagnosis, people would tell me to trust God. I continued to hear that phrase months after her death. I always had trusted God. His history with me was filled with trust-building moments. I never doubted that God could heal her or that He would. God wanted Jenny healed, too, right? After all, she was teaching Malaya, and a whole lot of other children to follow Jesus. Of course, He would showcase Himself for the children.

Trust God! I do! Well, I did.

Weeks after her death, I was on my back porch, which was a frequent place of prayer for me. I wanted to talk to the Lord about this trust thing. I knew my choices were to share some hard things with the Lord or to quit praying altogether. I knew this could be a pivotal moment in my faith journey, and I could feel the Lord inviting me toward Him. He was leading me on this dark, unfamiliar path, where I couldn't see the end or the dangers. But I was aware that there were things worse than coyotes and snakes.

I've heard it said that a child's first view of God is from their earthly father. For some of my friends/clients that is a blessing. For others, it has made the path to God extremely difficult. It doesn't mean you can't learn new things about God, it's simply your first impression.

My dad had decided to follow hard after Jesus right before I was born so I grew up watching him grow in faith. It was easy to ask my dad hard questions because he didn't have nicely boxed up answers. He taught me that there was nothing I couldn't ask him, as long as I watched my sassy tone. And I could have a *really* sassy little tone.

I had some things I wanted to ask Father God, and I knew I didn't want to be sassy. I wasn't angry with the Lord. I wasn't. Underneath what could've been my anger was disappointment. I was so disappointed with the Lord. I fully expected Him to heal Jenny and I *knew* He could do it. Could I have trust for Him after such deep disappointment? I *had* to talk to Him about this soul-crushing disappointment.

I am fully aware that He already knows the words on my heart before they are on my lips. While it seemed impossible to clean up the sassiness in my heart, I was more experienced in cleaning it up on my lips. He knows I love Him and do not have any desire to rebel against Him.

I stood up, pointed my head to the sky and asked, "You know I love you, Lord, and You know I want to be respectful. I want to trust You, but for what, Lord? What exactly can I trust You for? I need to know."

Oh my child, You will trust me to be who I said I am. I am always true to my character.

In His Names, we find His character. God is introducing us to Himself.

He is the Creator.
He is the Lord of lords.
He is the Great Reward.
He is the One who sees the pain.

He is the Provider.
He is the One who heals.

But here's a twist. Because of my desire to trust Him, I had to reject some of the language I've heard used in an attempt to package death up with a neat bow. We do not trust the Lord that everything will work out the way we want, that we will get our way. We live in a fallen world. Jesus said the power of darkness is the prince of this world. Not one of the apostles would've understood our language about following the Lord to get our way throughout life.

Suffering cannot stop us. Our language must lead us to protect our *no-matter-what* kind of faith.

So, trust Him for what? We trust Him to surround us. We trust Him to see us and to hear us. We trust him to give us exactly what we need to walk the path we are called to walk. We trust Him to use our stories for His purposes. Trusting God is essential to our direction.

> We lay our wounds at Your feet, oh Lord.
> We trust that You see us and that You hear us.
> We want to trust that You will clean our wounds and turn them into scars.
> We trust that You will redeem the pain.
> We will move through this darkness where we trust Your Light will be.

Blessed

I love the concept of "the blessing." It implies the Lord's spiritual gifts to us: His love, His presence, and His favor.

When Jenny went into the hospital, I had on a pendant that I wore every day for years. It read, in big letters, "BLESSED." I took that necklace off on the fourth day of our hospital stay to wear a picture of Jenny one her friends gave me. I had no idea how hard it would be to put that necklace back on. I would carry it with me wherever I went, wearing it for hours at a time. I would touch it, caress it, and wonder.

Was I? Was I blessed? I know I had been, but was I still?

To many people, the word *blessed* has come to mean more than God's spiritual gifts. It is now used to denote physical abundance, too. It has become associated with God's "muchness." For example, a bigger house, the raise, the bigger church, or the healing.

So, what does that mean when we don't get our way.

What if:
- The promotion went to your colleague, the one not as qualified as you?
- What if you worked hard on your marriage and your partner still leaves?
- What if instead of healing, there is a funeral? What then?

When we tie the word "blessed" with "muchness" then what happens to our faith when we don't get our way? It is a dangerous thing to link His love, His presence, and His favor with His muchness. Would the apostles have understood the way we use "blessing?" They understood what it means to receive spiritual blessings, to enjoy abundant life even in the midst of heartache and suffering. But when we teach that the faithful will always receive the external, physical "muchness," it can suffocate and destroy faith.

Let's say that on February 22, 2010, a mother pulls up under the awning of Baylor Grapevine Hospital and loads her daughter, with the balloons and flowers, into the car to take her home. At church that next Sunday, someone making the announcements says, "What a blessing it is! The Lord heard the cries of the mother's heart and blessed her by healing her daughter."

There's another mother that leaves Baylor Grapevine on February 22 to go tell a 9-year-old little girl that her mommy is gone. Is *she* blessed? If our definition of the word blessed includes God's presence, His love, and His favor, and getting our way, then what does it mean for someone who doesn't get their way? Are they void of His love, His presence, or His favor? And right here, some would write, "Asking for a friend." I'm not. My faith depends on how I answer this question.

I have worked with many, MANY couples who find this language so painful, especially when it comes from within our churches. People need to be able to go to their communities of faith to find healing language. A grieving client told me that after the funeral of his preschool son his pastor refused to speak of his death in their church again. "It will fill people with fear, and it goes against what I preach." I wanted to stand up in my counselor's chair and yell through the walls, "Then change what you preach!"

If it's not deemed a blessing and good, we won't discuss it? That is not the way of Jesus. He taught His disciples how to suffer. We have got to hit a pause button and think about the way we rattle on with flippant religious cliques that are suffocating the faith of the wounded.
Somebody, please say, "Truth!"

Too many grieving spouses, parents, and children walk away from communities of faith because of the way we use the word "blessing." Too many single people or infertile couples struggle to sit through the language of God's muchness. Why didn't they get the perfect partner or the beautiful baby?

I'm wrestling with the use of language around this concept too. But some things I know are:
- I don't have to hustle for the blessing of God. I already have it.
- I don't do anything to earn it. It is given to me to be opened and enjoyed.
- When it is truly a blessing, it will always draw me closer to Him. (Mmmm... Bigger house? Promotion? More money? This time, I'm actually asking for a friend.)

When God was introducing Himself to Abram, He said in Genesis 15:1, "Do not be afraid, Abram. *I* am your shield, your very great reward." God is *the* Gift.

My favorite verse about His blessing is Ephesians 1:3, "Praise be to our God and Father of our Lord Jesus Christ who has blessed us in the heavenly realms with every spiritual blessing through Christ."

Could it be that the best blessing of all is in the heavenly realms? That it isn't something we own or wear? The best blessing of all is that we have been given, through Jesus, exactly what we need to walk the road we've been called to walk, even when the road is full of bumps and crevices. Even when the scars from a wound leave me limping forever. I rearranged my dance moves to include the limp and the scar.

A small plot twist: About eighteen months after Jenny died, I began to wear my "Blessed" pendant again and it was stolen. Can you believe it? It was in my backpack, which also included my favorite marked-up, written-in grief book, my journal with all my dreams of Jenny. With the loss of those three things, I went back into hard grief. I wrestled with the Lord, then I made the definite decision to get on up; to claim my blessing. Without it, the power of darkness would be allowed to haunt me forever.

I am indeed a blessed woman. I enjoy the love, the presence, and the favor of the Lord, even though my story has a heartbreaking chapter. The scar is deep, but it holds the empowerment of His faithful gifts.

Hope

Three years before Jenny's death, I chose Psalm 71 as the focus of my year. It is the Psalm of Hope. Listen to some of the words the Psalmist uses, "You have been my hope, Sovereign LORD, my confidence since my youth ... As for me, I will always have hope; I will praise you more and more."

I had three years to memorize these verses and declare them with great passion. But then in February 2010, my hope was challenged.

Is there hope?

Well, is there? During those eighteen days, I refused to walk away from hope. I fought for every breath of it. But then, as we realized what was happening, on February 22, it felt like hope was being suffocated out of me. Every breath of hope was gone. Or was it?

Would I ever find a breath of hope again?

***

Through Jenny's struggle with secondary infertility, hope had become her favorite word. It had become mine too! We had gifted each other with lots of "hope" plaques, mugs, and picture frames. When I walked into her house after her death, and then into my own house days later, my eyes hung on every trinket bearing that word, but nothing could shake the void in my very spirit. Hope seemed so far away, so dark, and so deeply wounded.

The summer after Jenny's death, Rick was invited to speak at several churches. I listened to my man preach from Luke 24, probably a dozen times. And every time I heard something different. The Lord was teaching me about Hope.

Luke 24 is about two friends walking home after the death of their friend, Jesus. They are on the road to Emmaus, discussing, "everything that had happened." It is common for grievers to discuss every detail over and over, trying to make sense of it all.

"Did you see the way Mary was looking at Jesus?"

"Did you see the way Jesus looked at John when he asked him to take care of his mom?"

"Or the way John and Mary nodded at each other."

"Did you hear the Roman soldier?"

"And where was Peter?"

Jesus joined them on the road, but they don't recognize Him.

This couple didn't know about Jesus' resurrection, so they didn't recognize him when He joined them on their journey. He began to ask them why they are so sad. They are shocked that He was unaware of the events and asked Him how on earth could He not know about the devastation. "Jesus was our hope. Our hope of being freed from Roman oppression. Our hope for a better life. Our hope to peace. We believed him. We believed in him."

Catch this. They say to Jesus, "We had *hope*d that he was the one who would save us." Seriously, I envision them holding their heads in their hands and repeating over and over, "We had hoped. We had hoped. We had hoped."

They had hoped, been devastated by disappointment, and there He was, walking right beside them. Their eyes were blinded, but their hearts were burning. Yes, as they reflected back on the scene, they declared that their hearts were burning within them.

A few years ago, I was asked to speak on Hope. I was on a stage in Nashville, using the road to Emmaus story as my text when it hit me, right on that stage. I do not make a habit of working out a huge point after I'm already behind a microphone, on the stage. But I couldn't stop the outpouring of words as they formed within me: **"Hope is walking with me! The capital 'H' Hope is beside me, even when I didn't get my lower 'h' hope."**

Somebody stand up right where you are and yell, "Truth! Glory! That is truth!"

In my journal, I dedicated a page to the ongoing list of my lower case 'h' hopes.
    That Malaya would have faith.
    That she won't forget how much her mom loved her.
    That we would maintain a relationship with David.
    That David would stay in a walk with Jesus.
    That my sons and their families would be safe.
    That their faith would stay strong.
    That their children would profess and confess the name of Jesus.

That my marriage would survive this pain.
That we would both stay faithful to our commitment.
That my mind would live as long as my body (my mom died with severe dementia).
That my ministry would thrive.
That Rick would continue to enjoy his ministry.

These are all good things to hope for in this life.

However, I am not promised any of them. My physical eyes may not see these come true. At my death, there will be more of a comma than a period. I will not allow my heart to become so obsessed with my hopes not coming true that I miss the Hope walking beside me.

We've got to tell the next generation this, but only after we have believed it ourselves: There are going to be parts of our stories where we don't get our way, where our hearts get shattered, but our Hope of glory (as Paul calls him), the One who gives us our living Hope (as Peter calls Him) is walking with us.

I cling to Hope. As for me, I will always have Hope. My Hope has a name. His name is Jesus.

Hope is a powerful thing! It is air to the soul. It embraces excitement for the future.

***

Trust. Blessed. Hope.

Words are powerful! God used them to create the world. Jesus used them to heal diseases. We need them to recreate all that has been broken. Form your own. Press into mine.

Grief opened the floor of my heart to a new depth to everything. Everything. Definitions of the simplest of words plunge deeper. And sometimes, in the deepest of it all, there are no words, only groans.

Chapter 6
Grief as a Common Language
(JOSH)

There is a universal language spoken by humanity. You might be surprised by what it is.

I've traveled to a lot of places in the world, which means I've heard many different languages. There is a universal language that is common to every country, tribe, nation, and tongue. It's the language born out of hurt, suffering, and pain. It is **the groan**. For many walking the journey of grief, it is all they have. As my mom stated in the prior chapter, it's not easy to construct complete sentences when you're reflecting from the pit. It's hard to find the right words to accurately articulate the depth of pain the heart feels.

So, sometimes we are left with a groan. A moan. An utterance. A wordless sound.

And here is what is remarkable: According to the Bible, groaning is an effective, powerful form of prayer. Check this out:

[26] In the same way, the Spirit helps us in our weakness. We do not know what we ought to pray for, but the Spirit himself intercedes for us through **wordless groans.** *[27] And he who searches our hearts knows the mind of the Spirit, because the Spirit intercedes for God's people in accordance with the will of God.*[10]

Christian author and speaker Stuart Briscoe reflects on Romans 8:26-27 like this, "There is comfort in knowing that even the unspoken prayer of the uninformed opinion springing from the uninformed mind is valid when prompted by the Spirit who steps in and invests the sigh with significance and the tear with meaning."[11]

There are times we cry out, "God, all I have is this sound. It's the cry of a broken heart. I lift it up to you."

And from that, the Spirit of God declares, "I know exactly what to do with that utterance. Heaven can work wonders with that sound."

***

---

[10] Romans 8:26-27.

[11] Stuart Briscoe, *The Preacher's Commentary*, Volume 29, (Nashville: Thomas Nelson Publishing, 1982), 171.

In 2018, I traveled with a few dozen pastors to Ethiopia with Compassion International. Each day for a week we traveled to Compassion sites to visit with social workers, families, church leaders, and children. It was an incredible trip that opened my eyes to the transforming work being done through Compassion International[12] across the globe.

On our Sunday in Addis Ababa (the capital of Ethiopia), we were told by the Compassion team to meet in the lobby at a certain time because we were going to an English-speaking Ethiopian church. We imagined a church of 30-40 people and anticipated that our presence among them would double the size of their church for the day.

Church started at 10:00 a.m. We arrived at 9:55 a.m. to a warehouse that could seat a few thousand people. It was five minutes before worship was supposed to begin, and the place was packed! This doesn't happen in Memphis. People can show up to theaters and sporting events thirty minutes before they begin, but five minutes before church, they're still in the line at Starbucks.

For three hours we worshipped our hearts out. It was one of the most memorable worship experiences of my entire life. There were songs, testimonies, prayer time, confession, preaching, and more prayer.

At one point, the pastor stood up and stated the following, "Today, we have a tribe here with us. In Ethiopia, the roots of Christianity date back to the early days of the church. And today, the tribe that is with us has a tribal dance that dates back to the seventh century. I've invited them to share their dance with us."

My first thought was, "I definitely grew up in *white church*." In all the church events I've attended in my entire life, I don't remember a leader ever stepping up saying, "Today, we have a Christian tribal dance. Please center your heart in God as we are ushered into the throne-room of heaven." Quite the opposite.

I grew up in a church where you could get in trouble for clapping, hand raising, and swaying. The elders once met about raising hands, and they told the church that they decided it was ok if people wanted to raise hands, but hands couldn't go above the neck. It's a slippery slope, right? If they allow clapping, it will lead to swaying, which will lead to hand raising, and next thing you know we'll all be handling snakes.

---

[12] Compassion International. https://www.compassion.com.

Maybe you've heard the joke before: Why do Christians not make love standing up? The answer: Because it could lead to dancing.

Dancing just wasn't a part of my spiritual experiences before.

As the tribe gathered on the stage, I was anxious, nervous, curious, maybe even a little skeptical. But for the next twenty-five minutes, this dance captivated me. It held together in a short time every emotion you could imagine. There were moments when the pace was fast, hopeful, and full of joy. There were other moments when the pace was slow, sorrowful, and contemplative. There were moments you wanted to join by standing and shouting, and other moments you wanted to sit and lean in.

The dance had no tangible words. Just movement and expression.

But there was a sound. I'm not just talking about the sound of the instruments and feet moving along on the stage.

Throughout the entire act of worship, you could hear *the groan*. No matter the pace, expression, or emotion, you could hear a communal utterance.

And that sound touched down deep in the soul.

***

Witnessing this expression of worship led my mind to two places.

First, Barbara Holmes is the first one who introduced me to the language of **the moan.** It was a language that connected slaves as they traveled across the Atlantic to a new land. In her book *Joy Unspeakable,* she writes about how the journey from Africa to America was known as the journey across *bitter waters*; not because of the ocean, but because of the trauma. Chained to one another and spooned together lying on their sides, a language connected them. They came from different tribes and cultures, but on the ships, the moan became their common language.

Holmes describes it like this, "The moan becomes the vehicle for articulating that which can never be voiced ... moans are the utterances of choice when circumstances snatch words and prayers from bereft lips ... On the slave ships, the moan became the language of stolen strangers, the articulation of unspeakable fears, the precursor to joy yet unknown."[13]

In the same book, Barbara Holmes introduced me to the *ring shout*. This blew my mind:

> Although ring dances or ring shouts have particular significance for African communities, they were also recommended by Basil the Great, Bishop of Caesarea (329-379); Ambrose, Bishop of Milan (339-397); and John Chrysostom, Bishop of Constantinople (345-407). It was not until Augustine that dance as worship was converted from practice to analogy and metaphor. In all instances, the power of dance was recognized as an egalitarian expression that empowered the community and deepened their connection to God. "Dancing in the Judeo-Christian tradition is associated with the experiences that life is not determined by the past or the old self. Bondage to the past may be shaken off by dancing... In the Hebrew Scriptures ... dance celebrates and effects the end of slavery to the past and beginning of new freedom to act in the world and create a new community."[14]

It's believed that the ring shout was a distinctive feature of American black slaves, a vital expression of worship. Even in some places today, dance is the meeting ground for sacred and secular life. Through dance, bondage to the past is shaken off. The dance of both freed and trapped slaves was an expression of what was and what could be. It was highly communal, confessional, and anticipatory. What the ring shout — or ring dance — declared was that sometimes the language of movement expresses more than lyrics, words, songs, or sermons could ever do.

As the community would come together, someone would begin to sing, and whoever felt moved would step out of the circle of worshipers and they would begin to dance. Holmes says, "By chanting, dancing and clapping, the community provided a bass beat upon which the singer would create his or her own distinctive musical text."[15]

There were so many layers of meaning when considering the ring shout. They included pleading with God for deliverance, contemplative and meditative movements, and celebration from survival. It was inspiring, contemplative, evocative, and immersed in faith. From head to toe, they were all in.

As I read Holmes, I told myself that maybe this language was born out of slavery. Holmes didn't argue this point, but I began to create a narrative in my mind of God constructing a language that could hold suffering people together.

---

[13] Barbara A. Holmes, *Joy Unspeakable* (Minneapolis: Augsburg Fortress, 2004), 70-73, 75.
[14] Ibid.
[15] Barbara A. Holmes, *Joy Unspeakable* (Minneapolis: Augsburg Fortress, 2004), 70-73, 75.

Yet, after witnessing this Ethiopian tribal dance in all its emotion, intensity, and sounds, I realized I was wrong. The groan didn't begin in the bitter waters on slave ships.

The groan traces back hundreds of years to the ancient land of Ethiopia.

The groan was the sound coming from early Christians when they were torn apart by wild animals in arenas.

The groan is what could be heard from the Israelites in Assyria, Babylon, and Egypt.

It is the language that traces back to Abel's death in Genesis.

It is the language that was heard in the hospital when Jenny died.

It's as old as human brokenness. It declares that things aren't as they should be. Yet, in the sound is a strain of hope that things will be made right. It points to a day that is on its way when wrongs will be made right.

***

Secondly, as I reflected on this tribal dance I had experienced, I thought of Romans 8 and the groaning described by Paul. It's one of the greatest chapters in the Bible, and there's a lot of moaning affirmed in it. Creation groans. Humans groan. The Spirit groans.

Paul uses the metaphor of groaning as in the pains of childbirth (8:22). I chuckle when Paul uses this metaphor. I wonder how often he heard the pains of childbirth.

Comedian Jim Gaffigan jokes that during the birth of one of his many children, his wife groaned so loudly that it woke him up. I used this joke on Kayci during the birth of our second child. She didn't think it was funny. I'm curious how many women might approach Paul one day in heaven and say, "Hey man, loved your stuff. Ephesians rocks! Romans must have been a beast to write. I appreciate a lot of what you have done for the church. But I've got to ask, why multiple references to the pains and groans of childbirth? You don't even know!"

A lot more is happening in Romans 8 than groaning, but it's a consistent theme that can't be ignored.

And that's my concern today.

My concern (and fear) is that in our culture, we don't know what to do with the groans of people.

We want so desperately to silence the pain, to bring clarity to a crisis, to have answers for questions, and to alleviate heartache, that we will do anything to quiet the groans. We'd rather quickly process and diagnose the pain than sit with the sounds of suffering.

If you're familiar with the enneagram at all, I'm a 7. I love to experience life. I want adventure. I'm always up for a good time. I don't have to be the one who puts on the party, but I need to be at the party. I love joy, excitement, and happiness. Yet, the challenge for a 7 is that they suppress pain. Big time. We are more prone to addiction than any other number of the enneagram because we will do anything to escape pain.

Knowing this has helped me to mature as a pastor, and as a disciple. I've had to learn to embrace pain as a part of life as we know it. I can't numb it away, or suppress it forever, and I can't pastor a church to do the same.

We can't race through the cross to only focus on resurrection.

We can't skip suffering to get to adventurous discipleship.

We can't silence the groans of human hearts by telling people to just smile because heaven is going to be awesome.

Sometimes, we need to hear the groans coming from a person or a group of people, and then make the intentional decision to just sit with the sound. Honor it. Listen to it. Feel it with other people. Maybe even join in the sound yourself.

According to Romans 8, the Holy Spirit knows how to translate our groans into meaningful prayers that touch the heart of heaven. Paul doesn't say that the Spirit will pray for you when you don't feel like praying. We have to give the Spirit something to interpret. And the utterance from a grieving heart may be just that. An utterance. A short phrase. A word. A sound.

And God hears it.

God cares.

God speaks the language.

God knows exactly how to tend to it.

<u>**Chapter 7**</u>
Grief as an Optometrist
(Beverly)

Going to the optometrist is not my favorite thing to do. It feels weird, confusing, and a little helpless because you can't see what on earth they are doing while they mess with your eyes. Then there is the humiliation when they hold the basic letters and numbers up for you and ask you to name them. As a former teacher, I know the importance of knowing my letters and numbers. I want to get all of them right!

Not only do they ask you to name them, but they ask you to compare them: Which one can you see best: row 1 or row 2? 2 or 3? 1 or 3? I have to do each comparison a couple of times. I feel the pressure of getting it not only right, but perfect. This is all so I can see from a distance and read clearly for the next year, when it'll be time to do it all again. Just when you think it is all over, the doctor forces your eyes open and puts *those* drops in. Everything becomes cloudy and no one can tell you exactly when your vision will clear back up. Your eyes are super sensitive to light, so they give you wrap-around sunglasses.

Isn't that also the way with grief? There are questions, decisions, and confusion. What if we do it wrong? How long does the fog hover? Will we resist light forever?

What do you do the morning after your failed infertility test? Or the morning after the lunch that ends with a fractured friendship? Or the morning after the meeting where your boss tells you to pack your desk? Or the morning after the diagnosis (your own or someone you deeply love)? Or the morning after your husband or wife leaves or screams at you to get out? What do you do the morning after the funeral? What do you do the morning after it is your turn to have the worst day of your life?

What do you do when you're not sure what to do? In working through my own grief and having sat with hundreds of other broken hearts, I have learned that nothing is too basic. We have to get back to the letters and numbers. What once were the simplest of activities, now require focused intention to clear the fog from your mind's eye. There won't be a doctor there asking you which you can see better: 1 or 2, 2 or 3. You will be in the doctor's seat, however, trying to decide how to help your own heart see clearer.

***

Grief is like one huge, heavy ball. However, I found it more manageable to divide that ball into four smaller balls: Physical, Emotional, Relational, and Spiritual. I refer to these with the acronym PERS. These are four areas of focus for self-care. When emotional pain was/is intense for me, this checklist became part of my daily routine. And each day I ask myself:

- Have I done something to nurture my body today?
- What about my emotions?
- Is there anything I need to give myself permission to feel that I have kept locked away?
- Have I spoken kind words to another today, and have I opened my heart to someone else's encouragement?
- What have I done to allow my soul to be fed by the Lord?
- Have I practiced His presence?

These are disciplines I still practice over ten years after Jenny's death. I cannot envision that I will ever stop. Let's look at each a little closer.

Physical

When our hearts get broken, our bodies scream about it. Physical responses to heavy emotions compound emotional pain. With every sleepless night, anxiety builds. With increasing anxiety, anger soars. Eating takes on a life of its own. We either stop eating or gorge on sugar and crunchy carbs. It becomes a vicious cycle of chaos.

In the initial stages of grief work, we have to learn to take care of ourselves physically. Grief can produce a stress response in our bodies that actually lowers our immunity and makes us more susceptible to infections and serious illnesses. Here are important things we can do to focus on our own health.

Eating
Our eating patterns are often disturbed during grief. During this heavy anxiety, nausea, constipation, diarrhea, stomach pain are common. Eating well is never an accident, but especially not during this season. Choose healthy food options, more often, in smaller portions.

Sleep
Anxiety and grief are closely linked and they both upset normal sleep patterns. Some people report going to sleep fairly easily only to wake up startled a few hours in. Others report not being able to go to sleep. Good rest is an essential task.

It is important in both cases to explore your bedtime routine.

- No alcohol or caffeine within two hours of bedtime. Alcohol acts as anesthesia and doesn't allow for restful sleep. And caffeine fuels energy.

- Avoid anything with blue lights for one hour before bedtime. Blue lights are in any electrical device - tv, cell phones, and tablets.
- Warm baths (or showers).
- Journal three to five specific things you are grateful for from the day. For me, in the early days of grief, before I could get to gratitude, I had to journal some hard things. I call it, "emotionally throwing up on paper." I could sleep a little better in those early days when I wrote some of my questions, confusing thoughts, or scenes I needed to process. I equate it to when you have a stomach virus and wishing you could throw up because the churning in your gut is painful. That is exactly what it feels like emotionally following a painful event. Your gut is churning with confusion. Giving yourself permission to write is a helpful tool. Don't worry about spelling or punctuation, simply throw up on paper. (I don't use a pretty journal for the throw-up-writing. I throw it all away anyway. You don't go back and examine such things.)
- Read something relaxing. Maybe something predictable or that you've read before. When in stress, bedtime isn't the best time to learn. it is the best to still your mind.

We once believed that depressed people couldn't sleep. We now believe the opposite is equally true. People who don't sleep can become depressed.

Exercise
For physical health, the general rule of thumb is to exercise more days a week than not. When under emotional duress, mental health professionals recommend a daily cardio workout. Cardio workouts release endorphins and provide a release for your anxiety. Exercise can consist of power walks or crazy dancing in the living room—anything that gets your heart rate up.
Brain-imaging shows a positive change in the brain after a short twenty-five-minute workout. You deserve it!

Drink water
The goal is to drink half your body weight in ounces. Example: if you weigh 150 pounds, aim to drink 75 ounces of water. It cleanses the toxins that build in our systems when we are under significant stress.

Breathing
Listen to your own breathing. Grievers have a strong tendency to sigh and to yawn. Both temporarily turn off the stress response. Our bodies are not wired to take in deep, cleansing breaths when anxious. Our physical response to stress is preparing us

to save our lives through fight or flight. Slowing our breathing is central to any calming practice.

I encourage my clients and my friends to practice "box breathing." It is proven to decrease anxiety and stress, while increasing our mindfulness. It goes like this, take four seconds to breathe in, hold it for four seconds, breathe out (with noise) for four seconds, then hold for four seconds. Repeat until you become calmer. I can always feel it in my shoulders. You will feel the release whenever you hold your stress. Practice this pattern often so that when stress hits, it feels familiar. It works!

Crying

I want a sign for my office that says, "Tears are not only allowed but welcomed in this space." Tears can be a sign of bravery and authenticity. They can flow when we tap into the deepest place in our heart, the one that isn't visited often so it is raw and tender.

Giving ourselves permission to cry is a vital step in the grief journey. The tears of grief contain a different chemistry than any other tears. They contain stress hormones that are released when we cry. These tears also stimulate the production of endorphins, our body's natural pain killer and feel good hormones. Shedding the tears of grief is important to your health.

I wish I had a dollar for every time I've heard someone say, "I'm afraid if I start crying, I'll never stop." That, my friends, will never happen. You will cry. You will stop. You will feel better. You will repeat this process. Our bodies are equipped for this. Only when we become comfortable with our own tears can we really hold space for another's. The world needs more people who are brave enough to hold space with sorrow.

<u>Emotional</u>

Get curious

When I call a client from the waiting room back to my office, I typically ask, "How are ya?" I teach them that those words are a Southern greeting, to be answered with an "okay" or even a "fine" or simply respond back with the greeting, "How are you?"

However, then when I close the door to my office and we settle in, I will ask, "How are you?", with eye contact and compassion. A time of silence is appropriate while we sort through the possible emotions flowing. Grievers hate that question: *How are you?* Because we seldom know how we are. We are experiencing things we haven't felt before. We process feelings by naming them with mindful curiosity.

Emotions aren't positive or negative. But if feelings that accompany pain go unprocessed, the result can be negative behavior. You've heard it said that hurt people, hurt people. The more I am aware of my own emotions and work through them, the less likely I am to hurt another because of my pain.

Pain can mask itself in anger. Psychologist John Gottman says that often when we are angry, there are other emotions hidden underneath the surface. It is easy to see a person's anger, but it can be difficult to see the underlying raw feeling the anger is protecting. Stay curious. Ask yourself, "How are you?"

***

Don't numb. Do what comforts your soul.
When our family gathered for holidays before Jenny's death, everyone would leave on Saturday morning to get back to pastor their churches. Jenny knew that I was sad when everyone left so she would invite Rick and me to dinner. But that first holiday without Jenny, no one was coming back for dinner. I walked into the house, after running down the street chasing the cars in my robe (that's my Grammy tradition), and went straight into the kitchen pantry, closing the door. I wanted something crunchy. My eyes landed on my youngest grandson's Pringles. I don't like Pringles. I don't like the way they smell, taste, or the way they make my tongue feel. But they were crunchy. I had a personal contest with myself to see how many would fit in my mouth at once.

When I woke up from my chip-induced haze, I quietly opened the door and tiptoed to grab the Dustbuster to clean up the aftermath of my contest. Then, I found Rick and asked him if he wanted to go out to eat that night with friends.

Both of these events involved food. One was with silence, secrecy, and judgment; and the other, with sweet connections. One numbed my soul, and the other comforted it.

Any activity that gives us temporary relief from pain is called numbing. The list of things that numb us from pain can include, but is certainly not limited to, overeating, oversleeping, under-sleeping, too much alcohol, too much television, too many video games, too much social media, overworking, busyness, or anger. Numbing often produces regret and remorse when the activity is over.

Numbing doesn't just take away pain and discomfort, it takes away all emotion. When we numb, we will not experience happiness or joy. Numbing might temporarily ease pain, but it is not long-lasting, which leads to more numbing.

Finding and doing what comforts our soul is deeply rewarding and longer lasting. Give yourself permission to explore.

What could it be that comforts you? Is it reaching out to a friend? Cooking a healthy meal? Writing? Reading? Sitting in silence? Organizing something? Digging in the dirt to plant something? Exercising? Finding a new hobby? For me, the night I chose to break bread with friends rather than binge alone, my friends gave me emotional energy to continue to carry the pain. I still cried myself to sleep that night, but it blessed my soul to be with my friends.

Whatever comforts your soul, do more of that. I'll be eating Mexican food with friends.

Practice self-compassion.
Self-compassion is talking to yourself like you would talk to a friend. It is learning to be kind to you. it is speaking to yourself the way the Lord wants you spoken to, with gentleness and love.

Be intentional about how you talk to yourself as you figure out how to navigate a path you never would have chosen to walk. Speak encouraging words to you.

Give yourself permission to be where you are while also giving yourself permission to move into new territory. Give yourself permission to explore this deeper room of your heart.

Relational

Death changes relationships among those who are still living. People don't know what to do with those of us who have experienced profound loss. Our presence can bring confusion and discomfort. They don't know what to say. It takes bravery to walk the path of grief, but it also takes bravery to walk with a friend in grief.

In between Jenny's death and her funeral, Mike Cope, a friend and a pastor who has buried his young daughter, called my husband. He told Rick two things that have become increasingly important to us.

First, don't ever change your bio. You will always have three children. (We'll talk about this more in Part Three.)

Second, people are going to say some stupid stuff, but they are giving you the best they've got. Cover them with grace and mercy.

Every time I use this phrase, and I use it a lot, I picture myself under Niagara Falls where the noise is too loud for the words to invade my heart. In the offering of grace and mercy, and after a lot of practice, I'm learning to receive it myself.

People are afraid of grievers. Many of us are walking out another's nightmare. Our very presence brings pain, fear, and uncertainty. People are afraid to say the wrong thing. So instead of suffering through the humiliation of being wrong, they say nothing. But for us, the grievers, it is important not to make fun of another's best effort, but it is certainly okay to use your voice to teach a better response.

Please don't assume people are trying to hurt you. We are better people when we assume *good* - when we assume others are giving us the best they've got.

Use your voice. Just as you should not assume people are not trying to hurt you, you must also not assume they know what you need. They don't know what to say, and they don't know what you need. You know all those notes and texts that come early on, inviting you to let them know if you need anything? Make the call. Grieving is not the time to be independent. It takes a village to walk us through a hard season. Danny Mack says only you can do your own grief work, but you don't have to do it alone.

Give yourself permission to be with your *safe* people. Without exception, people who have found a healthy grief group report that it is the tool that helped them the most.

Practice kindness. Being kind is not the same as being nice. Nice is when I camouflage pieces of myself to make you like me. Kindness comes from a place of strength and bravery. In kindness, I can be open and honest, teaching people how to treat me. But love is flowing.

Good, safe connections calm stress. Good, safe connections help us carry our grief. Without them, our hearts will continue to suffer and ache. With them, we find sacred space.

Spiritual

Grief has the potential to bring up hard, spiritual questions. But the early days of grief are not the best time to work out theology. Everything about life, including the spiritual, seems so confusing. Our energy is best spent leaning into what we already know is truth.

***

In 2007, I was traveling home following a mission trip to Africa. I went as a counselor and a prayer warrior, and I taught a grief workshop. It was a fabulous trip of ministry and of pouring out our very souls. I know the Lord replenishes as soon as we give ourselves away, but let me just say, the replenishment hadn't happened yet, and we were boarding the plane for the journey home. As is common on mission trips, our desire was to travel as cheaply as possible. This meant long layovers and two middle-of-the-night flights. As we were about to board the flight from Chicago for the final leg home, I realized I didn't have an aisle seat, and we all wanted an aisle. There were sixteen women on this trip, and we sat like little ducks lined up one after another. It made getting up for frequent restroom breaks, stretching in the aisle, and sharing that "one more thing we need to talk about" easier.

I was told by the ticket agent that there was only one aisle left but it was in the very back, beside the restroom in the back of the plane. Fine with me! At boarding, I realized the seat beside me was empty. I settled in by opening a book and spreading African olive oil crackers out on my lap.

Just as the plane door was closing, a man came running straight toward me. I jumped up to let him in, spilling my crackers all over the floor, just outside the restroom door. I raised boys so I know about the five-second rule. For those of you with no sons, that means you have five seconds to pick up anything that has fallen on the floor, and you're good to eat it. It is said to take germs a minimum of five seconds to attach. I'm not sure if that's true, but that day I acted as if it was.

When I bent over to pick up my crackers, my about-to-be new friend bent over to help me. I expressed gratitude, and conversation began.

He was a professor in Japan who was on his way to the States to visit family. He had not been home for years and had missed the funerals for both his parents. My new friend had recently finalized his second divorce and wanted to see his brother and visit his parents' graves.

My friend: So, you're a Christian?

Me: Yes, I am! I love Jesus!

My friend: Oh, so you're a really passionate Christian.

Me: Yes! (remembering that he had been gone for a long time and because I say goofy things when I'm tired.) It's not just me! There's a whole bunch of us now!

Him: I used to be a Christian.

Me: What's the story?

Him: I was a youth minister. One Saturday night, I let the girls pray in a devotional, and in that church, it was a no-no. Girls could not pray out loud. The next morning, the preacher got up and looked at me as he started his sermon and said, "There are wolves among us." "I thought in that very instant, 'If I live through this, I want to run out of here and never come back!"

As soon as church was over, that is exactly what he did; he ran, as far as Japan, and never came back. He kept running, leaving behind all the things he was taught, including Jesus.
Then he asked me, "Tell me, why are you a Christian?"

Whoa! I am a Licensed Professional Counselor. I ask the questions. My brand new friend wasn't playing by the rules. I had just finished a week of ministering to missionary women. I am a pastor's wife. I have adult children who confess Jesus as Lord. It is one thing to be asked this question in Bible class while among other believers, but to be asked by someone who had walked away from faith … wow!

I am not a theologian, but I hang out with some. All I could think was to use really big words to impress the college professor. When I heard the word "propitiation" from my voice, I knew I needed to back up. Go simpler, Beverly. Use words you know what they mean.

"I choose to believe that the Jesus story is Truth. I choose to believe that somewhere in Israel there is an empty tomb. And that changes everything for me."

He said, "Where are you going when you get off this plane?"

My mom had taught me that was not a good question, so I said, "Where are you going when you get off this plane?"

I'm going home, to Decatur, Texas.

Wait, what!?!?!

That's where I'm going too! That is my home!

I bet you believe God gave you this seat.

I do!

I bet you're going to tell all your friends.

I am!

Neither of us knew I would be telling them for years to come or that it would be in a book.
For a few years, I thought this story was for my friend to get reintroduced to Jesus.

But when Jenny died, I knew this story was for me. I repetitively said when the way was so dark, "I choose you, Jesus! I choose to believe that somewhere in Israel there is an empty tomb. I choose you, Jesus."

Grief adds depth to the simplest of truths.

***

Exodus 14 has a story that I have leaned on heavily in this grief journey. When Genesis ends, the Israelites are on top of the world. Joseph is well respected and has brought his entire family into Egypt for food and prosperity. Then, there are approximately 420 years of the Lord's silence before the next book in our Bible, Exodus. When Exodus opens, the Israelites are now slaves. They are being beaten and abused. God breaks His silence to call His people out of Egypt and slavery.

But the Egyptians weren't ready to let go of the cheap labor. God began to roar in the form of ten plagues. We know that these plagues were for the Egyptians, but also for the Israelites. They were God showcasing His power. Finally, after the tenth and worst plague (the death of the firstborn), Pharaoh (the Egyptian leader) told the Israelites to get out. He said this in his own grief, immediately following the death of his oldest son.

It is a beautiful ceremonial story of the people of God leaving slavery and walking into freedom. It parallels the story of Jesus in the New Testament.

Now, in Exodus, Pharaoh cannot bear the deafening silence without the Israelite slaves. He gathers an army to pursue them. Just as the Israelites are beginning to feel the breath of this army coming for them, they arrive at a body of water, the Red Sea. They had never seen so much water. These people could not see the shore on the other side. They cried out to Moses. "Why did you bring us out of Israel? Didn't you know we loved being beaten? We loved pain." Isn't that the human way? We want to *go back*, even if it means going back to pain. At least it is familiar. We know how bad it hurt. We don't know what the future pain will be like.

Then Moses said these powerful words, "Stand still. The Lord you see will fight for you. Stand still and watch Him." Those verses are repeated in other contexts throughout our Bibles, but this is not the stopping point in this one.

The Israelites are saying, "We want to go back."

Moses says, "Freeze. Don't do anything. Watch God."

But then the Lord says, "Move on! I'm not going to do a miracle until somebody puts their big toe in the water." Sometimes God requires a movement of faith before He reveals His power.

When the Israelites stepped into the water, they still carried the scars of their beatings. They didn't walk in without their wounds, but with them. We don't *move on* away from our grief stories, but we *move on* carrying them. When we can't see the shore, we walk where we trust the shore will be. We turn our face into the direction of the Light of Heaven.

When you don't know what to do, do the next right thing, with your eyes in the direction of the Light of Heaven. Our eyes will see Him!

"So, we fix our eyes nor on what is seen, but on what is unseen, since what is seen is temporary but what is unseen is eternal."[16]

---

[16] 2 Corinthians 4:18.

***

For 44 years, I have been married to a man who is color-blind. Rick doesn't see pinks or greens. Our first house was pink, but he didn't know it until a neighbor told him. That's one way to get your house painted quickly!

Because he doesn't see some colors, for years, he missed some of my excitement over the beauty of spring. He remembers as a little boy being chastised by an elementary teacher because he couldn't name the colors correctly. It's because he couldn't *see* them.

But imagine his excitement when we heard of these new glasses to help colorblindness. We ordered them immediately and they came in a big box filled with colorful balloons. Our grandchildren were ecstatic to help their Grampy *see*. As each balloon was let loose, Rick's smile grew brighter. He could see colors!

After Jenny died, it took me months to see the brightness of color again. My eyes were clouded by the pain in my heart. But through physical, emotional, relational, and spiritual nurturing, my sight returned. In the deep place of my heart that grief carved, colors may be more vibrant than they were before suffering. I know I appreciate them more. Once you've been in darkness, light seems a bit brighter and a whole lot clearer.

Scarred Hope
Chapter 8—Grief as a Teacher
(Josh)

The weekend before COVID-19 began shutting down most of the United States, I traveled to Washington D.C. to speak at an event in Fairfax. I boarded my American Airlines flight with Group 4, took my aisle seat, and waited to see if a passenger was going to take the window seat next to me. Just before the door shut, a group of young college students ran onto our plane, and one young man made the motion to the window seat on my row. I stood to let him in. We proceeded to briefly introduce ourselves.

I noticed that he was struggling to get his seatbelt on. He couldn't figure out how to make the two pieces click together. Before asking to assist him, I realized I was most likely sitting next to a first-time flyer. I unattached my seatbelt and walked him through how to fasten the belt. I asked if it was his first time to fly. He said it was. He and a group of college students were traveling to Florida for a mission trip. For most of the students, they had never been on a plane before. You could tell by how big their eyes were. They were nervous, giddy, and frightened.

As we took off, my neighbor was like a small child. He elbowed me, "Man, you can see houses." Elbowed me again, "You can see cars driving on the road." Patted my leg, "Dude, you can see people playing in backyards." Then, he leaned back in his seat and put one hand on his stomach and said, "Uh-oh."

Now, if you know anything about me, my greatest phobia in life is throw up. I don't have a weak stomach. So, I'm not going to throw up if you throw up around me. I'm just going to run for my life while having no choice but to despise the throw-up-er for the rest of my life. I must admit, I'm better at all this since I've been a dad now for over thirteen years, but still, when a hand goes to the stomach and someone says, "Uh-oh," my first inclination is to grab a parachute and jump.

This time, I jumped into action in a different way. I pointed to the paper bag in the seat pocket in front of him, and then said, "Bro, this ain't happening. Not on my watch. Not today."

I patted his leg, "Look at me! Look at me!" He glanced over toward me.

I said, "Breathe. Lean back. Take a breath."

I did it with him. Together, we took a few deep breaths. And my friend was good for the remainder of the flight.

What was ironic, I traveled to Fairfax to speak at an event in which the theme was, "Breathe!" I felt really good about the content I carried with me into the event. David Fraze (a good friend of mine and well-known speaker) and I were speaking four times from Ezekiel 37. It's a vision the Lord gives the prophet, Ezekiel, and *breathing* is a significant part of the story. In the vision, there are bodies that look like they're alive, but they're not, because there is no breath in them. Preparing to speak on this specific topic was challenging for my own soul because often my pace in life isn't conducive to taking good, long, healthy breaths. I'm addicted to adrenaline. I love speed. I like to clip along at a fast pace. I struggle to understand why people don't want to move at my pace, but then I'm given feedback on how I make people feel extremely tired, because my pace in life isn't sustainable. It doesn't need to be repeated or mimicked. There is no telling how many times a day God is trying to get my attention by saying, "Breathe! Please, Josh! Take a breath. Slow down enough to catch your breath. Look at me! Breathe!"

I traveled back to Memphis where within five days, nearly everything in our country was shut down. Schools shut down. Churches suspended in-person gatherings. Restaurants pivoted to carry out or delivery only.

Over the next few days, I jumped on FaceTime with members at Sycamore View who were paralyzed with anxiety, fear, and paranoia. My message in my sermons and in pastoral interactions became the same message to the young man sitting next to me on the plane, "Look at me. Breathe! Take a breath. Center yourself in God."

***

When we're inducted into the grief journey, it can cause us to forget to do the simple things. This is why when people walk through divorce, miscarriages, the loss of a job, or the death of a loved one, people have to remind us to eat, get dressed, take a shower, and to do the simple things. The reality is we are off a little bit. We're not functioning at a high capacity.

As we navigate the storms of life, there is a God who walks with us, and that same God is eager to teach us valuable lessons about His heart, mission, character, and nature.

As we travel down painful roads, the last thing we may want to think about is pulling up a chair, taking out a pen and a pad, and leaning in to take notes from a teacher. A couple of months into our journey through COVID-19, I brought in a well-respected psychologist to talk with our team. She said that some psychologists argue that we're no longer going through a crisis. A crisis lasts about six weeks. After that, people deal with chronic stress. They also say that as we navigate crisis and chronic stress, we function at about 66 percent brain capacity. Think about it, COVID enough could do us in, but then add onto that social unrest, racial inequality, a heated presidential election, and all the emotions going into masks, protocols, and guidelines, and our entire society is walking on eggshells.

Yet, whether it is COVID, death, or relational dysfunction, God is eager to equip Jesus's church to faithfully walk through life as ambassadors for hope. God teaches through grief. Yet, students have to be prepared and willing to learn. I don't think it's that God takes us to school by causing us to suffer, but that God makes the most of teachable moments in order to refine character.

As God attempts to teach, God may not answer the *why*, but God diligently works to equip us for the *how*. Answering the *why* isn't God's primary agenda. Teaching us *how* to be faithful no matter what storms come in life is the work of the Kingdom of God. I don't believe God is behind every form of pain we experience in life, but I do believe that God can use whatever pain comes our way to teach our hearts about courage, joy, hope, adventure, and faithfulness.

There's no one who models this better than Jesus. There are two stories we've been given of Jesus navigating physical storms in life. Let's unpack these stories to see what Jesus has to say while in the storms, and how both experiences can prepare us to live life now.

***

Shortly after Matthew gives us the Sermon on the Mount, Jesus and His disciples got into a boat. All of the sudden, a windstorm arose, and we're told, "The waves swept over the boat."[17]

Last October, Kayci and I took a cruise with two of our closest friends. We cruised from New York City up the northeast coast into Canada. The final day was a sea day, and unfortunately, it was the roughest day at sea. A tropical storm had come up the East Coast, and we had to go through it to get back to New York City. The captain prepared

---

[17] Matthew 8:24.

us for the journey. He assured us that the boat could handle the waves. He shot straight with us though by informing us that the waves would be 20-25 feet. You know it's bad when the front desk informs the entire ship that free Dramamine is being offered for anyone who might need it. If you're in a car and you know bad weather is approaching, you can pull off the road and wait for the storm to pass. If you're in an airplane and experience turbulence, you know the pilots will work to find a smooth highway in the sky. However, if you're in a boat that is being battered by the waves, there is nothing you can do. It's not like 25-foot waves become 3-foot waves by moving the ship a few hundred yards to the right or left. You're stuck.

The irony in Matthew's story is that the boat is getting battered by the waves, but Jesus is sound asleep. Maybe the energy Jesus had poured into preaching, healing, and discipling had gotten the best of Him. Maybe it was a Sunday afternoon and Jesus modeled what a good Sunday afternoon nap was supposed to be like. All we know is that the disciples are freaking out thinking they're about to die, and Jesus is in the fetal position sleeping like a baby.

The rest of the story goes like this:
The disciples went and woke him, saying, "Lord, save us! We're going to drown!" He replied, "You of little faith, why are you so afraid?" Then he got up and rebuked the winds and the waves, and it was completely calm. The men were amazed and asked, "What kind of man is this? Even the winds and the waves obey him!"[18]

Notice how the story unfolds: They wake Jesus up. Jesus converses with the disciples. Then, Jesus rebukes the wind, which is the same word used to describe how Jesus drove out demons. Jesus uses energy and emotion to set wrongs right. Last but not least, when all things are made right, there is acknowledgement that the power of God has been displayed for them to see.

***

Matthew wasn't through telling stories about Jesus and storms. In chapter 8, Matthew is in the middle of telling stories in order to declare that Jesus is Lord over everything. In chapters 8 and 9, he strings together stories announcing that Jesus is Lord over physical diseases, social diseases, paralysis, fever, evil, demon possession, death, loss of sight, loss of the ability to speak, and yes, nature. There's nothing Jesus isn't Lord over. He is Lord over everything.

---

[18] Matthew 8:25-27.

A few chapters later, we find Jesus in a storm again. This time, Jesus had just been handed the news that John the Baptist had been murdered at the hands of Herod. In deep distress, Jesus attempted to get away from the crowd to be alone. I imagine Jesus wanting some space to mourn, grieve, and process life. Surely there was the terrible news of his relative John being beheaded, but there was also the reality that what happened to John, in a way, was going to happen to Him too.

As Jesus withdrew, the crowds kept coming. The next thing we witness is Jesus feeding thousands of people. Think about it, in Jesus' sadness, grief, and sorrow, He performs one of the greatest miracles told in the gospels. In fact, outside of the miracle of the resurrection of Jesus, it's the only miracle told in all four gospels. Just like Jesus, some of the best ministry that may flow from our lives are when we are in dark places too.

After stuffing bellies with fish and bread, we're told, "Jesus made the disciples get into the boat." I'm sure there were disciples saying, "Jesus, we don't do boats," or, "Jesus, give me a couple hours. I'm stuffed." But the command had been given, "Get in the boat!"

As the boat left shore, Jesus went up on a mountain to pray. Much like Matthew 8, a storm came upon the sea and the boat was being battered by the waves.

I've been to the Sea of Galilee, and I have witnessed how quickly a storm can come upon the sea. It doesn't take long for the Sea to go from being perfectly calm to battering waves.
Interestingly, the disciples struggled for nearly six hours, while Jesus stayed on the mountain praying. Most likely, Jesus could see that a storm had come upon the Sea, knowing His disciples were in the storm, yet Jesus chose to remain in the place of prayer until He felt released from the time He needed with God.

Early in the morning, Jesus began walking toward them on the water. In Mark's gospel, he writes, "Walking on the lake, He was about to pass them by..." (Mark 6:48). It's like Jesus was just taking a stroll.

However, in Matthew's gospel, a conversation ensued. The disciples think it's a ghost. When you're in the middle of a storm, it's hard to see straight; it's also hard to think straight. Jesus responded by saying, "Take courage. It is I. Don't be afraid."[19]

The next few verses are described like this: *"Lord, if it's you,"* Peter replied, *"tell me to come to you on the water." "Come,"* Jesus said. *Then Peter got down out of the boat,*

---

[19] Matthew 14:27.

walked on the water and came toward Jesus. But when he saw the wind, he was afraid and, beginning to sink, cried out, "Lord, save me!" Immediately Jesus reached out his hand and caught him. "You of little faith," he said, "why did you doubt?"[20]

I'm struck by what happens next. "When they climbed into the boat, the wind died down."[21] The wind and waves didn't stop until Jesus and Peter were back in the boat. Jesus could have calmed the storm before getting back to the boat. It would have made their journey back to the boat easier. I think Jesus wanted to teach Peter that with Jesus, we can conquer and navigate our way over and through the storms of life.

The disciples responded by worshipping Jesus, "Truly you are the Son of God."[22]

***

In life, rarely do we go looking for storms. The storms of life find us. We don't intentionally drive into the eye of a thunderstorm, tornado, hurricane, or flood. But each one of these will come upon us, most likely, in seasons when we least expect it. One day, the sky looks clear, and the next thing we know, we're in a storm and we can't find our way out.

I want to give you a few equipping pieces based on the two storms Jesus faced in his life. I hope this will comfort you in your storm, or that a nugget of wisdom will equip you for when the storms of life come.

First, the One who conquered the storm is the One who could have held back the storm. If Jesus had the power to make the storm stop, you'd think He'd also have the power to keep the storm from coming in the first place. This has baffled people and has caused all kinds of faith struggles over the years. Why does God allow storms? Why does God allow suffering to happen? God has the power to hold it back, so why?

I've come to believe that Jesus did not come to heal the world of disease, but to launch a movement that would transform the world. Until Jesus returns to set all things right, storms will remain a part of life as we know it. We don't ask for them, but they are part of the world we are born into. God does not orchestrate every storm, but God can prepare us to navigate it. God isn't the creator of every painful encounter that comes our way, but God is the sustainer of the weak, redeemer of the broken, and comforter for the afflicted.

---

[20] Matthew 14:28-31.
[21] Matthew 14:32.
[22] Matthew 14:33.

Secondly, in the storm, Jesus slept through one, and walked through the other. This isn't to say that Jesus didn't take storms seriously. However, there was a non-anxious presence about Jesus. He modeled how there can truly be a peace that can pass all understanding. Jesus was able to put the storms of life in their proper place. He knew they didn't get the last word. He knew they wouldn't last forever. He knew they wouldn't win. For Jesus, He refused to allow storms to define His identity or to have power over His life.

Thirdly, everything Jesus spoke was while in the midst of the storm. In the gospel of Matthew, if you have the red letters in your Bible, Jesus only spoke while the waves were battering the boat. In Matthew 8, Jesus asks a question about their faith. In Matthew 14, He assured them of who He was, and He conversed with Peter.

If you've ever tried to talk to someone while standing in a storm, it can be hard to hear each other. You have to yell in effort to communicate. As we travel through grief, pain, and even COVID, know that Jesus is diligently attempting to teach us while in the storm. Jesus doesn't wait until we get to the other side of painful events to sit us down and share wisdom with us; instead, Jesus speaks to us while we are navigating brokenness. For those of you currently engaged in the storms of life, listen for the red letters and the voice of God.

Fourthly, Jesus spoke directly to fear. Jesus doesn't want anyone to be taken down by unhealthy forms of anxiety, paranoia, or fear. As Jesus spoke during both storms, He addressed fear. He called His disciples to radical faith even when things seemed to be utterly out of control.

I can't help but imagine the power of these two stories in the lives of the disciples, especially Peter. I wonder how many times Jesus-followers found themselves in prisons, jail cells, and hunted by persecutors, yet they remembered that God had walked with them over and through the storms of life before, and that God would do it again.

I wonder if Peter would have the courage, bravery, and audacity to preach the way he did in the book of Acts if Jesus hadn't walked with him over the storms before.

Jesus doesn't deny that fear exists. I think Jesus acknowledges that there are a lot of reasons to be afraid. Yet, Jesus never wants to see His people taken down by fear. The mission of God is never put on hold or set aside. He continues through all seasons.

Fifthly, storms will pass. Storms are temporary. They will not last forever. Though there are times we wonder where the finish line is with COVID, suffering, or pain, we know that storms will pass.

Unfortunately, we also know that storms can leave a path of destruction behind them, and that life may not return to what it used to be. Our hope is in a God who will not let the destruction caused by storms get the last word.

Finally, our God will be worshipped. Both stories of Jesus navigating storms end with praise, honor, and recognition that God is fully alive and at work in the world. The disciples know that Jesus did the impossible. We can bank on the same too. God's not going to let storms get the last word.

As we walk through pain, I think one of the healthiest things we can do is pray, "God, I believe that you are bigger than this pain I feel. I believe that you will not leave me alone. I believe that you can use this season I am in to refine my character and to mold my heart. Do not let this season I am in rob me of joy, adventure, or courage. Speak to me God, your servant is listening."

***

A few years ago, I was flying back to Memphis late one Saturday. I had connected at the DFW airport and the flight to Memphis was only about one hour. Shortly after taking off for the 901, I moved over to the window seat. I typically prefer an aisle seat, but I had an entire row to myself, and I could see lightning in the distance. I wanted to get a better look at it. It was one of the most gorgeous lightning storms I had ever seen. With each strike it lit up the sky.

Then, something happened that I had never experienced before. I have witnessed lightning storms from the air. This time though, as we approached Memphis, we flew over the storm. The storm was below us. So, with each strike, it lit up the clouds beneath us. I couldn't see lightning bolts; I could only see clouds that lit up each time there was a strike. It was mesmerizing.

Then it hit me, if we were approaching Memphis, and there was a thunderstorm beneath us, somehow we had to get through a storm in order to land on the ground. I wasn't freaking out, but I did know that there was absolutely nothing I could do in the moment. I knew the pilot wasn't going to fly us through the eye of the storm. But I also knew that we were going to have to travel through part of the storm to land safely on the ground. I had to trust that the pilot had the training, wisdom, and expertise to navigate our plane through the obstacle in front of us.

The same is true for many of you reading this right now. It's like you are flying in a plane, a large storm is present, and all you can do is trust that God can help you get through it.

***

One thing I know is that if we want to learn in life, we have to be willing and prepared to be taught. Students have to wake up ready to receive from their teacher.

Grief has so much to teach us about faithfulness, character, integrity, loyalty, and passion. When grief becomes a teacher, it doesn't have all of the life's answers, but it works overtime to inject in us what it means to live a meaningful life even when we've been permanently marked by pain.

***

I hit a low spot in 2019. My morale and confidence took a major hit. It wasn't just one event that nearly did me in, but a combination of multiple events that collided in my life all at the same time.

I had a few friends who stepped up in my life to remind me of my calling. In many ways, they became the voice of God for me.

I began seeing my therapist more regularly. Dr. Katherine Blackney has been a gift of God in my life. She's a therapist who knows how to listen well, but she is also willing to ask hard questions that force me to process my pain.

As God often does, God also used the most unlikely people and the most unexpected moments to speak words of truth into my heart.

In September of 2019, I went to visit a friend of mine, Pat Simon, who was in hospice care. She had been given a few days to live. Pat had a remarkable story. For many years of her life, she was an angry woman. But the last ten years of her life, God renovated and reshaped her heart. She was a woman full of the Holy Spirit. The joy of the Lord permeated all around her. She had the gift of encouragement. Everywhere she went, people received a touch of God through her life.

I sat down next to Pat. Her arms were swollen. She struggled to breathe. Yet, she smiled and reached to hold my hand.

She asked me about heaven. We talked about it for a few minutes.

She shared with me again about how God had transformed her life.

We prayed together. I kissed her on the forehead. I told her how much I loved her. As I walked out of the room, Pat said, "Wait, Josh. I feel like God has given me a word to speak to you. Come back over here and sit down."

I had somewhere to be. I was scheduled to speak at a chapel service at the Harding School of Theology. However, if a dying woman tells you to sit down because she has a word of the Lord for you, you sit down!

She took my hand, and she said, "Josh, you have a tender heart. And tender hearts break easy. I bet your heart has been broken this year. God wants you to know that having a tender heart is a gift. It's a good thing. God wants you to know that whenever your heart breaks, God's not going to leave you broken. God will repair your heart. But right now, God wants you to know that having a tender heart is a gift."

A few minutes later when I got to the car, I sat there and wept.

***

I don't know exactly how God is going to teach you as you navigate your own storms. I don't know how God desires to reveal the love and power of Jesus to your heart. I simply choose to believe that God is eager to refine our character, to protect our joy, and to teach us how to remain faithful witnesses to Jesus no matter what.

So, let's breathe.

Lean back.

Take a breath.

Open your ears.

Let God speak into your heart.

Chapter 9
Grief as a Friend to Joy
(Beverly)

A few weeks after Jenny's death, our family gathered at our house. We found comfort in being together. We practiced giving each other space to ask the hard questions, even if we didn't have answers. We talked a lot and sat in silence a little. Both the chatter and the silence felt weird. Life felt so different without Jenny. We were trying to process it all, together.

Like most southern families, the kitchen is our gathering place. I don't remember what day, what meal, or what I was stirring when one of my daughters-in-law told me she had a question. The seriousness in her voice signaled for me to put my spoon down and to face her.

"Are you going to be bitter?"

Great question. I knew I needed an answer, immediately. Maybe not for her as much as for me. I'm not sure she remembers asking it. I will never forget answering it.

What could've been underneath that question?
- Will there still be laughter in this house?
- Are you still going to read books with the kids at bedtime?
- Will you still be a fun Grammy?
- Will there still be dancing in the kitchen? What about silly parties at breakfast?
- Will there still be sheer delight on Christmas morning?
- Or will bitterness gobble it all up and leave a putrid stink in its wake?

I knew the answer I wanted to share, so I said it quickly before I knew how I was going to live it out. They were simple words, yet had deep meaning, "Absolutely not. I will not become bitter." I said it with extreme conviction. Sometimes we all need to speak a Truth, then learn how to live like we believe it.

I don't know how yet, but I want to live into joy. Just like hope and peace, joy had always come easily for me. I have lived my life as a **glass half-full** kind of girl. Now, in the darkness that followed Jenny's death, I couldn't find the glass. Is joy obtainable for a grieving mother? Can joy be found by a broken heart?

***

Barriers create challenges, particularly when it's a barrier to something you really want.

For Valentine's Day, 2007, I wanted to get Rick, who had recently been diagnosed with high blood pressure, a healthy expression of my love. So, I chose chocolate-covered strawberries. A fruit, right? I was certain he would share. They're my favorite! I ordered them from *Prada Bistro*, a fabulous lunch place frequented mostly by women. I never went there to have a private meeting because the tables were close together, and I usually knew most of the people there, so it was like one big party.

However, not on this February 14. I could feel the silence before I even opened the door. There was a long line waiting to pick up delightful treats. The closer I got to the front counter, the silence was broken by spontaneous laughter in the kitchen. It was the kind that makes you smile even though you couldn't see what's going on. There was a glass shield separating the chocolate delicacies, and the sound of light-hearted laughter, from the long line of silent customers. There was a sign on the glass with bold letters, "Do Not Touch." Yikes! Everything, I mean EVERYTHING, in me wanted to reach under that glass and take a swipe at the icing on the first gorgeous cupcake. I wanted to be on the other side of that glass, with the joy!

Most of us walk through seasons where there seems to be a huge sheet of thick glass separating us from joy, from laughter, from the sense of belonging. I have friends and clients who share with me that the good things in life can seem elusive and far away. Unobtainable. There is a sense that joy is for other people, for the people who really belong, to the people who are worthy of belonging.

That, my friends, is not true. There is not a shield keeping us away, except in our own minds. We are free and even invited to take a swipe at the icing. We are invited to be in on the joy!

Joy is listed in what Paul calls the *Fruit of the Spirit*. In Galatians 5:22-23, Paul offers us a verbal snapshot of the very heart of God. The Fruit of the Spirit is love and when you open love up, there you find all the other delightful sections, like the carpels of an orange. When you open love, there you find joy, peace, patience, kindness, goodness, faithfulness, gentleness, and self-control.

Listen to the words of Paul to Timothy in 2 Timothy 1:14 (NCV), "Protect the truth that you were given; protect it with the help of the Holy Spirit who lives in us."

The Lord put part of Himself into the beating pulse of our own hearts. And where He is, so is His *fruit*. So, joy resides in our hearts!

Our hearts are just the size they already are, not getting any bigger. So, to make room for more of Him, we have to get rid of more of us (the things that don't look like Him.) In Paul's letter to the Ephesians, he warns the churches in Ephesus to avoid letting the devil get a foothold in their hearts. His toe can maneuver its way in when bitterness is allowed to grow. The seeds of bitterness are planted by pain, confusion, and suffering.

And that, my friends, is where spiritual disciplines come into play.

Spiritual disciplines are hard. They have to be practiced with mindful intention. Richard Foster shares in his book, *Celebration of Discipline*, "God has given us the Disciplines of the spiritual life as a means of receiving His grace. The disciplines allow us to place ourselves before God so that He can transform us. The disciplines are God's way of getting us into the ground; they put us where He can work within us and transform us. By themselves the spiritual disciplines can do nothing; they can only get us to the place where something can be done. They are God's means of grace."[23] Spiritual disciplines help us become who we are meant to be, receivers of His joy.

Here are four spiritual disciplines that are the pathway to finding and experiencing joy. This order can be changed, but this is the order that played out in my own journey.

- We decide to be brave enough to experience joy.
- We see our stories as a part of the larger story that began at creation.
- We practice the only pathway to joy, which is gratitude.
- We choose to enter the process of forgiveness: for ourselves and for others.

1-We decide to be brave enough to experience joy.

In December 2010 (only months after Jenny died), Dr. Brené Brown's work went viral following her TED talk on vulnerability. We were all mesmerized as she gave us words to discuss concepts that were already resonating in our hearts. I quickly became certified to facilitate her curriculum with others, particularly in grief groups. My tears flowed when she addressed joy as the most foreboding of every human emotion. Who would ever think of joy as scary? But it is, isn't it?

---

[23] Richard Foster, *Celebration of Disciplines*, (Downers Grove, IL: InterVarsity Press, 1983), 7.

As a young mom, Rick and I were given a trip to the Bahamas. It was a getaway without kids. I love my children, but this sounded glorious. I loaded one entire suitcase with books because I was going to do nothing but lay on the beach and read. In 1984, there was no limit on how many suitcases you could fly with or how much they weighed.

On the first morning, I picked out my book, slathered on sunscreen, grabbed a hat and sunglasses, and took off for the sand. I spotted the chair I was going to call home. Then, I looked up at the clouds; the moving, angry, dark clouds. I decided I would read in the rain, carefully positioning my book under my wide-brimmed hat. However, when lightning appeared, the lifeguard picked up my chair. I was disappointedly forced to spend the afternoon in my room, smelling like sunscreen. The next morning, I didn't allow joy to settle in until I saw the blue sky and beachy clouds.

We don't have to be very old before we've had hard lessons of joy leading to disappointment. Rick tells stories of the joy he experienced as a little boy when his alcoholic father promised to show up to watch him pitch in little league games. Rick would step on the mound and scan the crowd. No dad. Joy turned to painful disappointment.

Joy is scary because disappointment is incredibly painful. Many of us would rather forgo joy and live in perpetual disappointment than feel *that* pain. Yes, joy is hard. Joy is scary. Nobody knows this better than someone walking through a grief story. But, my friends, joy is worth it.

I want to be brave enough to silence the fear of disappointment that this could happen again. That someone else I love could die. You and I both know people who walk through multiple tragedies, but I don't want to show up for the dress rehearsal. The dress rehearsal can become more than a one-night event. It can become a lifestyle.

To avoid the dress rehearsal, we set our hearts on getting brave enough to quiet the voices of the fear of disappointment and hear the refreshing whispers (or roars) of joy. With bravery, we can open the eyes of our hearts to receive His gift of joy and then to put it on full display, not in spite of our brokenness, but because of God's grace.

A fill-in-the-blank expression that I began to use early on in my grief journey is, "I give myself permission to _____." I frequently wrote it on Post-It notes, placing them on my bathroom mirror, in my Bible, on my computer screen, or on my notes before I spoke publicly. I give myself permission to cry. I give myself permission to go slowly, speaking my truth. I also have to give myself permission to experience joy, to show up in the moments that settle my soul and in the ones that bring me delight.

Giving ourselves permission to experience joy is one of the bravest moves we can make. Joy can feel disloyal for someone in grief. There is an old grief adage that says, "It feels really bad to be so sad, but it also feels bad when you start to feel glad." After a death, it can shock us when we hear our own voices laughing or humming an upbeat tune. Our grief is a profound expression of our love. It is a brave move to allow that love to express itself through joy.

2-We see our stories as a part of the larger story that began at creation.

When we praise God, we recognize that we are living into a bigger story than our own. I struggle, like some of you, with controlling my thoughts during prayer. Not the minute-prayers throughout the day, but during the hunk-prayers when you pour out your heart. During my prayer time, I've been known to write the next sermon, a to-do list, or a birthday text to a friend. I don't feel the least bit of guilt about those things being involved in my prayer time.

However, sometimes, I absolutely crave the attention to focus on nothing but God. I have found this acrostic helpful in centering my mind and I am grateful I had lots of practice using it before intense grief hit.

I invite you to use **ACTSS** as a guide for prayer:
Adore Him - Praise Him for who He is.
Confession - Agree with Him about your mistakes.
Thank Him - Recognize the gifts from His hands.
Supplication - Make requests to Him.
Silence - Sit in stillness, listening for Him.

Separating *adoration* and *thanksgiving* was important for me. And not speaking a request until the third movement removes the ease of making prayer more like a wish list.

Psalm 63:1-8 is my Psalm. For decades, it has been my morning prayer. "Oh God, You are my God. Earnestly, I seek You. My body longs for You. My soul thirsts for You in a dry and weary land where there is no water. But I have seen you in the sanctuary and beheld Your power and Your glory."

His power is what He does. His glory is who He is. We adore Him for Who He is, and we thank Him for what He has done. When I was in the early days of grief, I couldn't see the goodness from His hand, but I could still experience the power of His glory. I could praise Him before I could thank Him.

Sometimes you just need to sit with who He is. You need to remember all the ways He has shown up in your history -- God's gracious fingerprints.

There was a song that I put on repeat for neighborhood walks. The lyrics were the language of my heart, drawing my hands straight to the Heavens, "Holy, You are still holy. Even when the darkness has clouded my sight."

Praising the One worthy of all praise is my reminder, my fuel, my energy, my joy, and my strength.

3-We practice the only pathway to joy, which is gratitude.

When the path feels dark, gratitude feels elusive, fake, and maybe even a little cheesy. But it is essential to our moving forward. Gratitude is a deep spiritual discipline. Grief opens up a depth in our hearts that we never knew existed. It is in that deep hole that a deeper gratitude can roam, and a greater joy can be mined, like gold in a cave.

Picture it, friends, you are in this deep cave in your own heart with a pickaxe in your hand, chiseling. With all the anxiety grief brings, you are able to chisel with energy. Suddenly your eye lands on it - a bright little nugget of joy. And with that, you catch a glimpse of gratitude.

Brené Brown says that "*every* participant (in her research on joy) who spoke about the ability to stay open to joy also talked about the importance of practicing gratitude." She said with that prevalence in the data, she committed "as a researcher not to talk about joy without talking about gratitude."[24]

It is impossible for our brains to experience anxiety and gratitude at the same time. Anxiety is so closely intertwined with grief that it is hard to tell when one ends and the other starts. But through the practice of gratitude, a different set of neurotransmitters light up in our brains and anxiety is quieted.

I want to encourage you to make practicing gratitude a part of your daily routine. It has become so important in my own life that I assign it to every client, no matter what the presenting issue may be. It is not simply an attitude. It is a lifestyle.

---

[24] Brené Brown, *Daring Greatly* (New York: Penguin Group, 2012) 123.

4-We choose to enter the process of forgiveness: for ourselves and for others.

I was teaching first grade while working on my master's degree in counseling. A mom of one of my students came up to me as the carpool line dwindled one afternoon. She asked me if I had learned any tips on how to forgive. She began to unfold heartbreaking stories of her childhood and the emotional abuse she was forced to endure from her father. I could hardly wait for her to finish so I could share all my wisdom. I think I waited for her to finish. I hope I did. Anyway, I detailed some beautiful strategies and waited for her to be in awe. Instead, she said, with all compassion, "My dad is dead." And at that, I was speechless.

Life gives us lots of opportunities to practice forgiveness. A death experience can bring even more. By death, I am referring to any death; physical, a broken relationship, death of a dream, etc. This list could go on. These events produce what the therapeutic language calls "unfinished business." *Unfinished business* is awash in the "what if's."

What if we had gone to the doctor sooner?
What if I had driven and not him?
What if we had moved away after the affair?
What if I had paid attention to the warning signs?
What if he had been emotionally healthy and knew how to treat a little girl?
What if...?

These questions are like rocks in a backpack. They get heavier and heavier over the years. They can eat at the very fiber of our hearts and make them weak. And, maybe most importantly, they squelch our joy.

Before we can define what forgiveness is, let's look at what it's not.

Forgiveness is not:

Forgetting it. Our brains are not wired to forget deeply, painful events. They will still pop up at the least expected moments. That doesn't mean you haven't forgiven.

Condoning it. There may have been real mistakes made. Things that don't make sense now and will never be understood. Things you would never do again. We often ask "Why?" when there is not a reasonable explanation.

Trusting again. Forgiveness and trust are very different even though they can hold hands. Forgiveness is an act you can do all by yourself whether the other person apologizes or changes. It is a gift you give to yourself and to another. But trust is always earned. I can choose to forgive someone that I will never trust.

Reconciliation. Reconciliation takes at least two and is dependent on mutual response. Forgiveness takes one.

What forgiveness is:

A choice. Forgiveness is a choice to release the pain of *unfinished business*. The first step is usually to decide to forgive. Sometimes we have to begin by praying to *want* to forgive.

A process. Forgiveness is not a cheap phrase we use to deny the pain and move on. It is better to say, "I want to learn how to forgive you." We recognize this is a part of a sacred journey and absolutely not a one-time event.

A release. Maybe it's the release of a dream, or the release of control. Maybe it is the release of the marriage you've had, or to build the marriage you want. This release frees you to really live. It is not saying the wound wasn't costly or that it didn't matter. It is saying I can't be who I want to be while carrying this much pain, resentment, and/or bitterness. Becoming obsessed with these events robs us of joy.

***

Defining forgiveness is tough. I've known people who had words of definition and never practiced it. I've known others who practiced it but couldn't find words to define it. The practice is more vital than the definition. Words of definition give us a starting spot to practice. Forgiveness is not a denial of pain, but an acceptance of transformation.

Desmond Tutu, in *The Book of Forgiving*, says "With each act of forgiveness, whether small or great, we move toward wholeness. Forgiveness Is nothing less than how we bring peace to ourselves and our world."[25]

With our special person's death, we may have to forgive them, or maybe forgive ourselves. With the physical death of a special person, there is forgiveness of an

---

[25] Desmond Tutu, *The Book of Forgiving* (New York: HarperCollins, 2015), 6.

unfinished conversation or one-sided love. Forgiveness is required when we have been wounded by another or when we experience remorse or guilt that we can't release easily.

Without forgiveness, we are more likely to go on wounding others without even recognizing that we are the ones with a sword or a verbal machine gun. Without forgiveness, we believe we are always the victim. With forgiveness, we come to recognize the strength of the Spirit's work in us. With Him, we are more than conquerors. With forgiveness, the chains of bitterness are cut and the pathway to deeper joy is ours.

Whoever is the object of your forgiveness, I want to share a couple of ideas I offer to my clients. The Bible invites us into at least two dramas that remind us of what the Lord has done in our hearts, in our souls, and for our lives.

One is baptism. God invites us into this beautiful ceremony that Paul outlines in Romans 6 as the reenactment of the death, burial, and resurrection of Jesus. Because it is something we *do*, we remember. We have a date to know when we chose to enter into our new life with Jesus.

Another is the Lord's supper, also known as communion, or the eucharist. We do this to remember the gift of Jesus, God-in-flesh coming to earth, and joining His Spirit to ours. Through this, we remember His history and we claim our future with Him.

To do the deep, hard work of forgiveness, sometimes we need an activity to remember the moment we chose to enter into this process. Here are two ideas to help us remember the moment we entered the process of releasing pain.

One idea is that I have my clients gather some small rocks and head to a body of water with a Sharpie. Write on those rocks the sin or the hurts they are wanting to release, recite Micah 7:18-19 while throwing those rocks into the water, picturing the pain attached to that rock.

Who is a God like you, who pardons sin and forgives the transgression of the remnant of his inheritance? You do not stay angry forever but delight to show mercy. You will again have compassion on us; you will tread our sins underfoot and hurl all our iniquities into the depths of the sea.

This is from a Jewish ceremony called the *tashlich*. Once a year, the Jewish people would - and many still do -- go to a moving body of water and empty the trash from their pockets as they quoted this verse. They watched their hidden sins or secret sins be washed away never to be thought of again.

I had a client who had lived in secret sin for years. After he confessed these secrets to his wife, followed by a season of separation, they decided to repair the marriage and start fresh. As part of his recovery, he took some rocks and headed to a river, inviting his wife to join as his witness. After watching him for a while, she asked if she could borrow that Sharpie and then found some rocks nearby. Forgiveness is contagious.

The second idea is to remember the moment we chose to release the pain by writing out the details of the pain. Then, go to an outdoor fire pit or grill, placing the pain in the fire, watching the smoke rise to the Heavens, while quoting Revelation 8:4, "The smoke of the incense, together with the prayers of God's people, went up before God from the angels' hand."

We picture the Lord receiving our pain. God knows more about what happened to us than we have a clue. He sees it. He knows it. He can redeem it. He is the Giver of Joy.

Forgiveness is a vital component in all grief. It refuels our energy to open our hearts to joy.

***

A few years ago, I was in Memphis and joined Kayci for a Bible study called *Downline Ministries*. The speaker captured my heart with her story. When she was in her early 20s, she was dating a man, making plans to marry him. When he told her that he did not want to follow Jesus anymore, she made the difficult decision to walk away from the relationship. She believed, totally believed, that the Lord would send her another man because of her faithfulness. She focused on looking for "him." After a decade, she realized that God might not be sending her another man. At this point in her story, she paused, then quoted John 10:10 with striking conviction. Hear the words of Jesus, "The thief has come to steal, to kill, and to destroy. But I came to give life - life in abundance."

For the woman struggling with infertility - you can have life in abundance.
For the man or woman who has never married - you can have life in abundance.
For the one who had to file bankruptcy - you can have life in abundance.
To the one who has a tough diagnosis - you can have life in abundance.
To the grieving mom or dad - you can have life in abundance.

***

On Jenny's first birthday after her death, I knew I didn't want the pain of her death to overshadow the joy of her birth. I want to remember the life of Jenny Laine Bizaillion with joy!

Here is a piece that Jenny wrote in a prayer journal that she passed back and forth with a friend; a friend also in a secondary infertility battle. It now hangs in *Jenny's Hope*. It hangs where I see it multiple times every day. I never want to forget the wise words of a beautiful young woman who died way too young. Following her death, I found a Joy worth fighting for; a joy that would hold hands with my grief.

> God, rip us constantly of "self." And fill us back up with attributes of you.
> Just like Moses, may we never get complacent in one place.
> May we never stay in place of SIN, GRIEF, ANGER.
> Give us a strength and a constant desire to move,
> to walk forward, to keep journeying.
> May we experience our indescribable, unexplainable JOY.
> May we be clay. And we beg of you, God,
> to never stop your work in us until you bring us to perfect completion.
> Do WHATEVER it takes in us and in our families' lives
> to bring us completely to you!
>
> Written by Jenny

***

In our waiting room, right where the door opens into my view, I had an inscription placed as a reminder to me: "Grief and Joy can hold hands." I want Joy to be in the middle of the sentence with a capital letter so that I can be reminded that my Joy is Jesus. He is the One who understands my grief and gives meaning and purpose to every ounce of the pain. Someone once asked me how I can say that and teach that we can't experience two conflicting emotions. Grief and Joy are not in conflict, my friends. They are both rooted in love.

Grief and Joy can hold hands.

Introduction to Section Three
Ten Conversations (A Dialogue between Beverly and Josh)

My mom and I love conversations. We live for them. Though my physical features reflect my dad, my personality is like my mom. We are extreme extraverts. We're addicted to adrenaline, action, and enthusiasm. People have joked about the two of us that if you were to tie up our hands before preaching, neither of us would be able to speak in complete sentences. We very much enjoy our lively conversations.

Section 3 of our book is going to function like a dialogue. In fact, that's how this section came about. We sat down together, turned on our voice memos app, and recorded ten conversations. We have taken you on a journey through this book that has been narrative (Section 1), instructional (section 2), and now we want to equip and inspire through dialogue (section 3).

Preparing for this part of our book made me think through how conversations between my mom and I have evolved over time. In the 1990s, once I began maturing in my faith, our conversations often centered on what a personal relationship with God looked like. Books like *Experiencing God* by Henry Blackaby, *The Purpose Driven Life* by Rick Warren, and *Intimacy with the Almighty* by Chuck Swindoll were flying off bookshelves and capturing bible study groups all over the country. Though in different stages in life, we both wanted the same thing, a deeper prayer life focused on intimacy with God.

In the 2000s, our conversations shifted to the unity of the church and justice in the world. Though neither of us had ever been held captive by legalism, God began opening up our eyes to the many ways God works in the world. Through some of my encounters with God through service and compassion, God began revealing how much His heart bends toward the oppressed, marginalized, and forsaken. Our conversations seemed to be about how God is reconciling the world, and that more people were invited to sit at the table in Jesus's Kingdom than we ever realized.

Since the 2010s, our conversations have mostly centered on hope, grief, joy and pain; not necessary in that order. Though we have experienced grief before, the death of my sister Jenny sent us searching for answers. When we couldn't find answers—because grief tends to provide more questions than solutions—we found that good conversations were like medicine for the soul.

When my mom and I have deep conversations, it usually involves sitting, finger foods, and either coffee or a glass of wine. We settle in, toss out a question or topic, and then we go for it.

So, we invite you to join us. Pour you a drink. Get comfortable. Join the dialogue.

Chapter 10
Does Time Heal?

JOSH
Mom, I am thrilled that we have included this section in our book. I'm ready to go. Here's the first of ten conversations. You ready?

BEVERLY

I couldn't be more ready. I have my sweet tea and chips and salsa next to me. I'll try not to crunch loud. I'm wearing my *Jenny's Hope* shirt, so I'm dressed for the occasion. Rick is watching the Golf Channel, so I don't anticipate him interrupting me for a few hours. Let's go.

JOSH
First question: *DOES TIME HEAL?*

It's a phrase you hear all the time in grief. Whether you've lost someone close to you, recently experienced a divorce, or any other crisis, people will often say, "Time heals." So, does it?

BEVERLY
No. It doesn't.

JOSH
Well, way to ease into it, Mom. I know you knew the question was coming, yet you still chose to begin your response with a definite "no." Why?

BEVERLY
Let me say it this way, I don't believe time heals. However, I do believe time done well heals. But let me backup and explain why I don't use the phrase "time heals" for my own grief journey or when I'm counseling people on theirs.

Early on in my grief journey, I went through a phase where the word "healed" bothered me. For a while I couldn't figure out why. Then, it became clear why the word made me shudder. We heal what is broken. We need to be healed, because something needs to be fixed. So, if I need to be healed because of my loss, does that mean something is wrong and broken? If so, what exactly is wrong and broken? Is it wrong for me to miss Jenny and want her back? Is missing my daughter something that needs to be fixed?

With the phrase, I'm afraid it may set people up for false hope as if the day will come when grief will be no more. It's not something that's going to happen on this side of eternity.

JOSH
I've said for over a decade that grief doesn't go away. It takes on new shapes and forms, but grief doesn't go away. It lingers. It is part of us. And I don't think this is a bad thing.

With that said, time can have its way with us. If we're led to think that "time heals," when there are setbacks on the grief journey, we can easily become frustrated. As a culture, we like progression. We are enthralled with progression, which means we like to move toward a goal. If the goal is complete healing, and then we experience a season that feels like a setback, it can throw us completely off.

BEVERLY
I've lived that. And anyone who has walked a grief journey has felt that too. We may have a few good months, and then wham! We're flooded with memories or the overwhelming sense of loss.

I want people to know that healing is a process. We settled on the name for this book—***Scarred Hope***—because the image of scars has given us a powerful reminder that the scars we bear are memories. Healing does not mean that we forget. It means that we remember well.

JOSH
Mom, we settled on the name of this book because my first book was named ***Scarred Faith***, and in a way, this is Part 2. Right?

MOM
Really? You really want to go there right now? I bear scars on my body because of you. This is where I would put a smile emoji to let people know that we are laughing, but this is a published book.

JOSH
Just trying to make you crack a smile for a minute. I'm a 7 on the enneagram, which means when things go too deep into pain, I try to make people laugh.

Seriously, grief doesn't have a finish line. We want the pain to stop, and we would like to know where the finish line will be. When will the pain be over?

We're having this conversation in the spring of 2020. Covid-19 has brought the world to a near halt. Many are struggling psychologically because we don't know where the finish line is out there. When will it be over? When will the current *time* we are in be over?

BEVERLY
Exactly!

So, let me reiterate, I do not believe that time heals, but I do believe that time done well will bring forms of healing. As healing occurs, we will learn to carry the pain.

There's a movie from a few years ago starring Nichole Kidman.

JOSH
Eyes Wide Shut? Mom, that was a rated-R movie.

BEVERLY
NO! Not that one. And quit interrupting me. It was called *Rabbit Hole*.

In the movie, Nicole Kidman's character, Becca, had a young child run out into a street, was struck by a teenage driver, and died. Her brother passed away in his 30s from a drug overdose.

JOSH
Good grief! What a nightmare. I don't remember this movie.

BEVERLY
It was released around 2010. If I remember right, it didn't make a lot of money in the box office, but Nicole Kidman won multiple awards for her performance. It's a great movie for understanding grief. I don't recommend it for couples looking for a nice romantic night together.

There's this scene where Becca and her mom are standing in an attic. Now remember, Becca's mom had to travel a grueling grief journey too.

Becca asks, "Does it ever go away?" She's referring to the pain. She's asking, "Does it ever get easier?"

Becca's mother responds, "No. It changes though."

Then, she talks about carrying the pain. The image she uses is that it's like someone sews a brick in your pocket. No matter how hard you try, you can't get the brick out. But one morning you wake up and forget the brick is there. Then, you go to put your hand in your pocket to get a tissue out, and you remember the brick is in there. You may forget the brick is there, but when you bump into the kitchen counter, you remember.

That's what it means that time done well heals.

It means you learn to carry the pain.

JOSH
I'm undone. That image is so powerful!

The truth is that we grieve hard because we love hard.

BEVERLY
Shortly after Jenny passed away, my grief therapist encouraged me to pay careful attention to the vocabulary I used for grief. Instead of saying, "I'm grieving Jenny hard today," say, "I'm loving Jenny hard today."

The only other thing I would add is this, growing up, I was taught that 1 Thessalonians 4:13 declared, "Grieve not." It was often taught like a command, "Don't grieve!"

Now, I see 1 Thessalonians functioning so much differently, and better. Instead of hearing it as, "Grieve not." I think it is saying, "Grieve. Go for it. But know that as we grieve, we don't go about it like people who don't have hope." Hope and grief are companions on this journey. They need each other.

JOSH
I've heard you say before that you believe Jesus wants us to hold space with our pain. In other words, don't sweep it under the rug.

BEVERLY
Exactly!

JOSH
Time done well heals.
Healing doesn't mean we forget.
We can learn to carry our pain.

BEVERLY
Truth!

Chapter 11
Does Everything Happen for a Reason?

Josh

Our goal throughout this book, and especially in this section, isn't to make people feel bad for things they've said to people in their pain. One time in my late teens, I told a man who was walking the road of infertility with his wife that he just needed to hang on like Abraham and Sarah. Seriously, I used Abraham and Sarah to try to comfort him in his pain. My comfort-narrative I chose in the moment was to keep holding on and maybe this baby will come when you're 90 or 100.

Beverly
Oh, Josh. I crack a smile listening to you say that because, well, it wasn't a comforting thing to say. I'm sure the man gave you a blank stare.

Josh
That's exactly what he did. Just stared.

Beverly
I'm sure he did. However, I also smile because I've been there too. We've all been there.

Josh
I know we have. Our goal right now isn't to scare people to the point they don't want to say anything because they're afraid of causing more hurt, but to equip people that when they do speak, they will weigh the impact of their words.

Beverly
I like that, "Weigh the impact of their words." In the clinical world, we talk about helping people *hold space with their pain*.

Josh
There's a phrase most of us have heard countless times throughout our lives, "Everything happens for a reason." Neither of us like this phrase. We resist using it as we pastor and counsel people. We don't like when others have used it with us. But why? What is it about this phrase that makes us push against it?

Beverly
A hundred faces scroll through my mind when I hear the phrase, "Everything happens for a reason." Time and time again it has thrown my clients into a state of confusion. People who speak this phrase to those in pain, typically do so with conviction in their voice. It's often said with an air of resignation. Or more accurately, it's often said with a feeling of defeat.

Josh
YES! Almost as if someone is trying to defend and protect God.

Beverly

Exactly. But this is where we have to be careful. There are verses in the Bible that support this idea.

Josh
Yep. Ecclesiastes 3:1, Romans 8:28, Hebrews 12:7, and there are others.

Beverly
Yet, this idea is not consistent with the overall theme of Scripture. It isn't consistent with the character of God.

Josh
More specifically, it isn't consistent with the character, behavior, and nature of Jesus. I think I can speak for us both in saying that we believe that Jesus depicts what God has been like all along. If you want to know what God is like, look at Jesus! Jesus didn't come to reveal a new side of God. Jesus wasn't heaven's PR strategy to repair God's Old Testament reputation. This is what God has always been like.

Beverly
Absolutely! Jesus' way of engaging the brokenness of the world wasn't to begin by trying to insert meaning, but rather Jesus began by inserting His presence. Jesus didn't step into pain to explain in, but to be present in it. This was a game-changer for me when God opened my eyes to this.

Josh
That is so good! Jesus shows that incarnation often comes before education. This God-with-us promise comes before Jesus-the-teacher. But with that said, we do have a hunger for meaning in life. We want life—our lives—to have meaning. We don't want anything, especially death, to be in vain. Yet, the good news of Jesus holds back from explaining away every form of pain as *everything happens for a reason*, and instead, it offers mystery. The gospel offers mystery. There is mystery to so much that happens in life. We want so bad to believe that God is working everything for good, but this doesn't mean that God is orchestrating bad in order to make things good.

Beverly
In John 9, Jesus is asked, "Who sinned. This blind man or his parents that he was born blind?" Jesus responds by basically saying, "Wrong way to think about this. That isn't how this works." There is mystery. For Jesus, he dismantled religious clichés. He still does this today. Don't live on clichés alone. We have something so much better to offer people and the world.

Josh
Maybe another way to frame this conversation is this: *How does God's sovereignty work?* We believe that God is sovereign, but what do we mean by that? I believe God is sovereign over this story that we are in. God is sovereign over the outcome. God is sovereign over the beginning and the end. But with that said, I don't believe God is sovereign in that God orchestrates every event, action, and moment of existence. God doesn't pull strings. This isn't a show for God. Life before and after the fall in Genesis 3 was a life in which God was desperate to connect with His people and with all of creation. Where some people may differ is this: Some choose to believe that God's glory drives God more than anything else. I tend to lean heavily toward the belief that God's covenant love is what drives God more than anything else. In Jesus, we discover that God—in God's sovereignty—longs to connect with people and creation no matter what circumstances and forms of pain we find ourselves in. Therefore, God doesn't design, orchestrate, and plan for pain, but because there is pain, God works to redeem and restore what has been broken. This is what drives me in my life, ministry, and faith.

Beverly
I could not agree more. Here's how I talk about Jenny's death, the birth of *Jenny's Hope*, and the work of God: Jenny didn't die so Wise County could have a grief center. But since Jenny died, Wise County now has a grief center. There is a reason and meaning in her death, but it didn't precede her death. I truly believe that God is too creative to need a 31-year-old wife and mother to die in order to launch a grief center. Yet, I also believe that God is creative. Let me rephrase that, God is *redemptively creative*, so that God passionately worked through a death to bring an opportunity for healing to the county.

Josh
"Redemptively creative!" I like that a lot! Did you think of that on your own?

Beverly
I'm sure I got it from somewhere, but I'll take credit for it today.

Josh
I'll give you credit the first time or two I use it in a sermon, but after that, it's all mine. That's how it works.

Beverly
Oh yes, I know. I've been married to a preacher for over thirty years.
Any other thoughts about the phrase: *Does everything happen for a reason?*

Josh
Thanks for keeping us focused. Yes, one more thought. While I don't believe everything happens for a reason, I do believe *everything happens*. What I mean is, *life happens*. Throughout life, we will be inducted into clubs we never asked to be a part of. Divorced, widowed, bankruptcy, loss of a child, etc. This isn't because God places us in each one of these clubs, but because life happens.

Beverly
Life does happen. And we are inducted into clubs we never cared to be a part of. Even for those who may read this chapter and not agree with our dislike of this phrase, I'd like to encourage them to be careful and thoughtful if and when they choose to say that everything happens for a reason. Use this phase with care.

Josh
I've seen this phrase cause deep pain, especially with those who have endured forms of abuse. I preached a sermon back in February of 2019 on sexual abuse. For those who have had to travel the journey of betrayal, abuse, rape, and the trauma that attaches to such tragedies, there is no redemptive reason for such things happening. Everything doesn't happen for a reason. So, yes, we must be thoughtful, responsible, and caring how we speak to those in pain.

Beverly
I don't want people to take the road of avoiding those in pain because they don't want to say the wrong thing. I do want to encourage people to keep learning how to speak the language of grief. We can do this.

Josh
Yes we can.

Chapter 12
How Many Children Do You Have?

Josh
Ok, mom, you have three children. There's not another one I'm unaware of, is there?

Beverly

That is correct. Three children. And no, there isn't another one out there somewhere. Three babies have come out of this body. Jenny was born August 3, 1978. You were born September 12, 1980. Jonathan, June 25, 1983.

Josh
Rank the three pregnancies from easiest to most difficult.

Beverly
I know you've heard me say this before, but the summer you were born was the hottest summer in recorded history. I think 2011 beat it, but oh Josh, it was so hot. And to make things worse, the air conditioning broke in our car that summer. We hardly had any money. We had one car. I would carry cold wet rags in the car to put on Jenny when we had to drive around Abilene.

Josh
I think every year I live that summer gets hotter.

Beverly
Don't mess with me. It was miserable.

Josh
For years when our family would be together throughout the year during holidays, birthdays, or family vacation, Jenny, Jonathan and I would have fun joking about who was the favorite child. Typically, we make arguments for ourselves. Since Jenny died, those jokes aren't as funny.

Beverly
I get that. Especially early on, we had to learn how to laugh together as a family again.

Josh
I'll give you and dad this, you didn't play favorites with us growing up. Now as a parent, I know it can be a challenge to give equal time, attention, and love to each child. You and dad did that very well.

Beverly
Thank you for speaking that over us. I'm sure if we could go back there would be things we would change, but I definitely receive those words of affirmation.

Josh

I want to ask you to tell a story. A few months after Jenny's death, dad was a guest speaker at another church for an event being held on a Wednesday night. You traveled with him. It came time for a bio to be read during the introduction. Well, you take it from here.

Beverly
I was not prepared for this moment. I thought I was, but I wasn't. This is a church that was very familiar with our story. Rick had spoken there in the past. The minister of this church was out of town that night, so another staff member had been given the assignment to introduce Rick. It started like you would imagine, "We are so glad to have Rick Ross with us tonight." Then, he began reading Rick's bio. Now, keep in mind this is a bio that Rick had given them to read. "Rick is the Preaching Minister at the Decatur Church of Christ in Decatur, Texas. Rick and Beverly have been married for 34 years. *They have two children and four grandchildren.*"

I almost yelled, "Excuse me!"

Josh, I almost came out of my chair. I grabbed Rick's leg because he was still sitting next to me. However, Rick wasn't paying attention to the introduction. He was looking at his notes. I didn't know if I should raise my hand to correct the mistake or if I should just remain silent. He was wrong. That's not what Rick's bio says. The minister changed it in the moment, because he didn't know how to speak of Jenny's death. He didn't mention Jenny at all, and there was no mention of Malaya. The man walked to the back of the room and Rick stepped up to preach. I almost chased the man to the back, but I thought that may not be the right thing to do. So, I sat there an emotional wreck. "*Do I just have two children now? No way! No! I refuse to believe that.*"

Josh
You called me after that event. It was a moment you were definitely confronted with the reality in life that so much has changed. Within minutes after Jenny died, we both had conversations with Mike Cope. I spoke with Mike in Memphis as I drove home to pack our bags to head back your way in Texas. And you and dad spoke with Mike from the hospital as you were preparing to leave. Our conversations were similar. For those who may not know, Mike and Diane Cope lost their daughter, Megan, when she was 10. They've had to walk the journey of grief in the past and have become close companions to those of us who have had to walk grief-journey since. He told us to be prepared to offer grace to people. He was aware that people would soon say foolish things in an attempt to offer hope and healing. He prepared us to offer grace, because people are giving their best in the moment. But, he said something else to you and dad. What did he say?

Beverly
You're right. Mike called within minutes after Jenny's death. He shared with us what you just expressed, and then he said this, "Do not change your bio. You will always have three children. Do not ever change your bio."

Josh
So, what does your bio say now?

Beverly
It says this:
Beverly and Rick (her husband) have three adult children and five precious grandchildren. Jenny, their daughter, died in February, 2010. Since then, Hope has been an intentional focus of her counseling ministry. Romans 15:13 is quoted at the end of every event at WCCC. She is clinging to Hope, Joy and Peace.

It does not suggest that I used to have three children, but that I have three children.

Josh
I've heard you talk multiple times on the importance of language. This has come up throughout this book on numerous occasions. We have to learn to speak the language of grief and pain.

Beverly
More specifically, we've got to learn to use death-language. It is not an easy language to speak. The associate minister who read dad's bio wasn't an evil man with malicious intent in his heart. He didn't know how to speak death-language. It isn't just death-language, but loss-language. How do we talk about something precious that we have lost? With the launch of Jenny's Hope, I spend a lot of time with people who have lost loved ones to death, but I also spend time with clients who have lost marriages, confidence, dreams, and so much more. We struggle to know how to speak about these things. Do we hang pictures of our loved ones, or do we not hang them? Do we mention the ex-spouse when we tell the story of our lives, or do we leave them out? Do we hang Christmas stockings for the loved one who has passed, or not?

Josh
I should know this, but do we? Do you? Do we hang a Christmas stocking for Jenny?

Beverly
Yes. I do. It is there for us to remember. It gives voice to our story.

Josh
When children die, whether as small children or as adults, one challenge I often hear is that the deceased can become perfect in death. What I mean is that we can idolize them by stripping away their imperfections and lifting them up as spotless angels. Has this been a challenge for you with Jenny?

Beverly
For the first year or so after Jenny's death we were just trying to survive. Well, we were trying to survive and attempting to keep Malaya moving through life. That was our focus. When your dad and I began thinking through the kind of people we wanted to become on this side of Jenny's death, we made a conscious decision to not idolize Jenny. It isn't fair to Jenny, to the story of God's work in her life, or to the rest of the family.

Josh
You and dad have done a really good job of that.

Beverly
Let me say this too, it is very hard to be a parent and to grieve. I didn't lose a young child, but even in losing a 31-year-old daughter, it has been very hard to be a parent and grandparent and to grieve. I encourage women and men every week at Jenny's Hope, do not lose who you are in this story. Be present where you are. Sadness is going to be with you for a long while, but you do not have to let sadness rule your life.

Josh
I want you to end this chapter with a declaration.

Beverly
What do you mean?

Josh
Declare for us right now who you are. What is your bio?

Beverly
My name is Beverly Ross. I have been married to Rick Ross for 45 years. I have three adult children. I have five precious grandchildren. Hope has been an intentional focus of my counseling ministry. I cling to Hope, Joy and Peace.

Chapter 13
Don't Be Sad; She's in a Better Place

Josh

Mom, let's dive into a discussion we have had dozens of times over the years. All grievers have had statements made to them that seem insensitive, inappropriate, and often just ignorant. And, to be honest, most of us have made those statements too. What phrases come to mind as you think about this topic?

Beverly
Oh, Josh, there are too many to count. I've heard "heaven needed another angel," "God needed her more than we did," and, "Jenny would want you to be happy."

Josh
I try to live a life committed to non-violence, but when certain phrases are mentioned to others experiencing deep pain, my non-violent tendencies begin to break down. I need people to remove themselves from a six-foot radius of me. It's not that I need them to practice social distancing so we don't get each other sick, but because I need some space to keep me from causing bodily harm.

Let's talk about this one phrase that we've all heard before in one variation or another, **"Don't be sad; she's in a better place."**

Beverly
A couple of thoughts:

One, there is a physical reaction every single time I hear this. It is not a statement that has ever brought me comfort. It has never brought me peace in my pain. It has never nurtured my heart in moments of despair.

With that said, I feel the need to make something very clear. Yes, there are phrases we have all heard that don't help others, but I want us to be very careful as we critique things to say and not to say to those who are in pain. We don't want to make fun of these statements in a way that makes people want to stop talking. I'm afraid if we point out what people shouldn't say in a way that makes them feel inadequate, ill-prepared, or even like they're a failure when it comes to walking alongside those who grieve, that ultimately people will stay away from grievers. This isn't what we want. We need to give others, and ourselves, permission to say the right things, and to say the wrong things. Does this make sense?

Josh
It does make sense. I'm glad you took a moment to speak into this. Anyone who has heard you speak over the past decade has heard you talk about being able to cover

people in grace and mercy. I think this would be a good time for people to hear you speak a little more into that. Do you mind sharing what that has meant to you?

Beverly
I know we mention this in a couple of other places throughout this book, but when Jenny died, Mike Cope called Rick. I know he called you too. In a short conversation, Mike made sure to make two things clear: 1) don't change your bio. You'll always have three children. 2) When people say stupid stuff, they're giving you the best have. Be prepared to cover them in grace and mercy.

So, Josh, you know I'm a high-energy, animated person.

Josh
Of course, I do. You handed it down to me.

Beverly
I do this thing when I need to cover people with grace and mercy. I literally raise my hands to eye level, and I make this motion as if I am covering myself with grace and mercy. It's my way to cover myself and to cover others with grace and mercy.

Josh
I bet you wish you had that exercise in your life when you were raising me.

Beverly
Which time? When you kicked in the back door because no one was home and you left your key in the house? Or maybe when you threw the football in the house and broke my glass vases?

Josh
As for the backdoor, over time, I have come to regret that decision. As for the glass vases, I threw a good pass. Jonathan dropped it.

Beverly
Yes, I'm sure this grace-and-mercy exercise would have been helpful as a mother with children in the home. Yet, for our conversation happening now, it has been a discipline that God has given me to center my heart. It forces me to take a deep breath. It reminds me that the person in front of me is often giving me the best they have to give.

Josh

I think what bothers me the most about phrases like, "don't be sad; she/he is in a better place," is that it asks people to deny their pain. Now, with that said, I do think there are times when the statement is true. When someone peacefully passes away at the age of 95, their absence may sting, but there can be great happiness and joy that they are in a better place. There is no more pain and suffering. They rest in peace and rise in glory. I don't feel the same way about other deaths.

Beverly
I feel the same way. When my mom died in 2013, there is no doubt in my mind that she was in a better place. Dementia had set in. She was comatose. Her death was her gain, and we were all ready for her to be released from pain and suffering.

However, Malaya tells a story about Jenny's funeral. Remember, Malaya was nine, and somehow after the funeral while all the adults were scattering talking to people, Malaya got separated from her family. She remembers someone telling her, "Malaya, be happy. Your mom is in a better place." Malaya remembers feeling frightened and scared. She didn't know what to say. She just remembers that it didn't sound right.

Josh
That's right. Sadness is an emotion that was created by God. It's okay to channel it every once in a while. I've heard you say this many times, that we have to learn to hold space with our pain. We have to learn to give space for others to hold their pain. There are times I have people ask me to pray that we will be strong and not show emotion. I gently try to correct them. I don't want people thinking that sadness is a sign of weakness or lack of faith. It's not. It's a feeling and expression of loss.

Beverly
Holding space with our pain is a phrase I use often at *Jenny's Hope* and in my own life. At Jenny's visitation, Randy Harris, Diane Cope, and Brady Bryce drove in from Abilene to spend a few minutes with us in Fort Worth. I remember standing with them, and I said this, "I can't imagine Jenny being happy right now." It wasn't that I thought Jenny was miserable in the presence of Jesus, but that Jenny wouldn't want Malaya or David to have to walk this journey. When I said that, any of the three of them could have attempted to correct me or to redirect my comments. They didn't. Randy looked down at the ground. Diane just stared at me. Brady looked past at the wall behind me. No one said anything. They held space for my pain.

Josh
What a gift! You'll never forget that.

Beverly
I never will. At times, it's the best I have to offer others as well.

Josh
We want to give people freedom to feel whatever it is that they feel. If we don't give them that space we unintentionally rush people into acceptance.

Beverly
In the clinical world, we often say, "If you don't feel it, you can't heal it."

Josh
I like that.

Beverly
Me too.

Josh
I think I want to leave people with the beauty and power of Revelation 21:4. The same verse that ends by stating that there will be no tears in heaven, begins by declaring that in heaven God will wipe tears from faces. We serve a tear-wiping God. And this is very good news.

Beverly
Yes, we do. And yes it is great news.

Chapter 14
How Do You Cultivate a Healthy Marriage While Grieving?

Josh

Mom, let's talk about marriage. Specifically, let's talk about how couples cultivate a healthy marriage while also traveling the journey of grief. Now, we have acknowledged multiple times throughout this book that the grief journey encompasses a lot more than just death. It could be bankruptcy, loss of job, life transitions, becoming empty nesters, or the stress of reaching the age where you're caring for your own children and your elderly parents. The grief journey doesn't have only one entrance door.

Talking about empty nesting, you and dad had a rough time when you became empty nesters, right?

Beverly
Are you kidding me? We have never had so much fun in our entire lives. Every night was a party. Well, until 9:00 p.m. when your dad would go to sleep. But seriously, we raised you three to get out of the house and to make a life for yourself. We adjusted well because you three adulted so well.

Josh
So, you're saying I've always been mature?

Beverly
I don't think that's at all what I just said. But thanks for the laugh.

Josh
Back to cultivating a healthy marriage while grieving.

Beverly
Yes. As for cultivating a healthy marriage while grieving, yes, let's go deeper. This is vitally important. To begin with, we don't come into marriage as individuals with blank slates. By the time people enter into a marriage covenant, they've already lived two, three, maybe four decades of life. Wounds and scars have had their way with us. We come into marriage with backpacks full of past experiences that have played a major role in forming the way we interpret pain and life. Whether you like or not, these things are a part of us.

Josh
I often tell people that there are days when marriage is the easiest thing in the world, and there are days when it is the most difficult thing in the world. We must choose marriage every single day we're in it; not just the day of our wedding.

I'm a huge proponent of what you do, mom. I know the counseling services you provide is more than marriage counseling, but I also know that's a significant part of your work. In marriage counseling, especially when there is a need for reconciliation, two people have to be willing to name the chasm. Reconciliation means that there is brokenness and that distance has been created. We can't skip the process of naming what it is that caused the pain and separation. We have to name it for what it is in order to get to a healthier place. However, when grief enters into a marriage, we have to pause to attempt to name potential chasms that could cause separation. We've got to take a breath and say, "Look, we're in for a tough journey. Let's talk about the potential roadblocks, obstacles, and challenges that could potentially find their way into this covenant. Let's be proactive and prepare for it now."

Can I get a, "Truth?"

Beverly
Truth!

Josh
I've always wanted to use your phrase, "truth." Not bad. Did I use it correctly?

Beverly
You did. Not bad.

Josh
Is it true that divorce rates are higher when a married couple suffers the loss of a child?

Beverly
You hear that a lot, though I'm not sure there is research to back it up. David Kessler says it like this, "Child loss is not what causes divorce but rather judgment of each other's grief is what causes divorce." I often say it like this, I'm not sure if the death of a child promotes or leads to divorce, but it can rob you of joy and energy to hold it all together.

Josh
WOW! That's rich!

Beverly

Two people with empty tanks can't fill each other up. It doesn't work that way. This is why it is necessary for two people to know what fills the other's tank.

Josh
Kayci and I work hard to do that. As you said, it is necessary to know what fills each other's tank. We grieve differently. We don't handle stress the same. To use the image you painted, we don't pull up to the same type of gas pumps to fill up our own tanks. One spouse may prefer Exxon; the other prefers to use points at the Kroger pay-at-the-pump.

Beverly
Absolutely! Your dad and I grieved differently, but we found ways we could grieve together. After Jenny died, Rick and I would take a lot of walks. There were times we would hardly talk. That may not surprise you because you know your dad doesn't talk much in the first place. But we would do it together.

Josh
When Jenny died, Truitt was two and Noah was six-months-old. We were grieving, but we also had two little ones relying on us to nurture them from the moment they woke up until they went to sleep at night. I won't lie, Kayci picked up the slack. I'm sure I wasn't a good parent for a few months. However, when the kids went to sleep, Kayci and I watched *Friends*. We didn't really watch it when it ran from 1994-2004, but we watched all ten seasons in about two months. It's not the most wholesome show, but it provided us with many laughs, and in a way, it became our therapy.

Beverly
Your dad and I watched reruns of *Everybody Loves Raymond*. It's a show we know really well. We knew it had provided us with laughs and connection in the past, and we trusted that it could give us needed laughs again. It didn't disappoint.

Josh
I totally get it! Not only do Kayci and I grieve differently, we handle stress differently too. For example, when Kayci is stressed, she wants to take a nap. And you know how long Kayci can nap. I joke that my wife doesn't nap; she hibernates. As for me, I want to work out. It's a stress relief. She goes to bed. I go to the gym.

Beverly
I've always been so proud of Kayci's ability to nap. She's one of the best I've ever seen do it.

One of the hardest things for Rick and me in 2010 was that we weren't together every night. I immediately stepped into Malaya's life to nurture her the best I could. I spent many nights at David and Malaya's house. So much of my attention and energy was going toward Malaya, I just didn't have much to give to Rick. That was a challenge for us, and it was something we had to talk through multiple times. We realized that though Malaya needed me, Rick did too.

Josh
I know you have a few principles you like to share when you wade into this conversation with clients and friends. Do you mind jumping into those?

Beverly
Absolutely! Here we go.

Stay each other's student. You cannot assume you know what the other person is thinking or doing. In grief, and in life for that matter, health rarely comes through assumptions. Both partners must be willing to teach the other, and to listen when being taught.

Josh
Kayci sometimes asks me to listen to her with my eyes. Give her my attention.

Beverly
Truth! There is so much wisdom in that. Especially in grief, it is hard to be taught, and it is also hard to express what you want because a lot of times we don't know what we want. So, here's what I encourage people to do: give ideas of what we might need. For me, there were times I had to tell Rick, "Ok, Rick, when I cry, I want you to try this...or that..." I didn't know what I needed. I wanted to give him options of how to respond. Then, maybe we would both discover what actually provided comfort in the moment or not.

Josh
I love that, Mom. **Stay each other's student.**

Beverly
The next is this: **Stay curious**.
There are times when you have to be able to ask each other, "What are you thinking right now?" No one needs this question to be asked twenty times a day, but there needs to be space, especially in a marriage, for us to ask these types of questions. When we do, the listener needs to be ready to receive. They don't need to become the

miracle-working therapist in the moment that attempts to fix everything. They need to be the curious partner who genuinely wants to understand their spouse.

Josh
Stay curious. Ask questions. Ask open-ended questions. Curiosity is such a gift.

Beverly
Here's another one: **Give each other permission to do it differently.**

After Jenny died, I began hanging pictures of Jenny all over the house. I wanted memories of her to be evident everywhere I went in my house. One day Rick finally asked, "Beverly, how many do we have to hang?" Of course, Rick wanted pictures of Jenny in the house. But it was also overwhelming. We had to talk about something as small, yet enormous, as how many pictures to hang throughout our home.

For me, the 22nd of every month was a really big deal. It has been since Jenny died on February 22. For Rick, it wasn't a big deal for him, but because it was for me, it became a big deal to him too. I have a friend, Liz Moore, who texts me every month on the 22nd. As we sit here having this conversation, there have been 125 "22nd's" since Jenny passed away. I have received 125 texts from Liz. Because it is a big deal for me, Rick acknowledges this too.

Rick loves to play golf. It is his safe place. I don't play golf, but I would ride in the golf cart with him when he went to play.

Josh
This is such a good principle to have, because we are all wired differently. However, I've got to ask, golf is supposed to be a game with very little talking. Is that hard for you to not talk much when you're out on the course?

Beverly
Extremely!

Josh
Sorry for digressing.

What's next?

Beverly
Last but not least, **Be comfortable with each other's tears.**

Man's number one fear is shame.

Woman's number one fear is isolation.

Men feel shame when women they love are stressed or in pain even when it doesn't pertain to them. They want to fix it. That's what they seem wired to do. They want to step in and make it better.

Unfortunately, some have been raised to believe that tears are a sign of weakness. For most of us, we don't know what to do when we're with people crying. It can be awkward and uncomfortable. But a lot of times when people cry, they don't need to be fixed. They need to know it is ok for them to release some emotion. They need to know it is ok.

Josh
Be comfortable with each other's tears.

Beverly
Practicing love toward another is soothing to our souls, even when in grief. To practice love, I found myself asking, "What would a loving person do here?" And then I worked to do more of that. Grief changed both Rick and me, but we refuse to let it steal our love.

Chapter 15
Should I Seek Help?

Josh

As we begin a chapter on seeking help, I think I should begin with two statements. 1) You and I are both proponents of therapy. For you, it is your job. For me, it's closely connected to my job. We believe in counseling. We recommend it. We are for it.

Beverly
I would agree with that.

Josh
Statement #2 is this: I have a therapist. I have had one since 2013. She is a gift in my life. It is one of the best decisions I have ever made for my mental health and emotional well-being.

Beverly
You have shared that with me over the past few years and I'm very proud of you for taking that step. I hear from clients and people we serve all the time who express how difficult it was for them to pick up a phone and call our office. It was even more difficult to actually walk into our space for their first appointment. Becoming vulnerable is risky. To get well when your own heart or a relationship is broken is not easy. Sometimes, it is easier to suppress the pain than to open up in order to get to a better place.

Josh
That's it, mom! That's it, right there. Let me go all theology, preacher-mode on us all real quick.

Beverly
Ok. Go for it.

Josh
In John 14, Jesus gives instruction about the nature and function of the Holy Spirit. One of the primary roles of the Holy Spirit is to be a counselor. The Holy Spirit desires to work in our lives in order to equip us to reflect more of Jesus in the world. As the Holy Spirit works to sanctify and transform us into the image of Jesus, our hearts and minds must become open to the working of the Spirit. Therefore, I believe that good, trained, equipped therapists function as agents of the Holy Spirit. Can I get a "truth"?

Beverly
Truth!

Josh

Easier said than done. As you said earlier, reaching out for help is a risk. It's a difficult move.

Beverly
I think acknowledging that is a good first move. Now, let me make a couple of points. I want these points to be helpful. There are different tiers as we reach for help. One question asked in pretty much any form of therapy is this, "Am I going crazy?"

Josh
Mom, I've been there. A couple years ago, I was going through a rough patch. I reached out to my therapist and that's exactly what I asked of her, "Hey, I need you to tell me right now ... how messed up am I?"

Beverly
Well, now I want to know what she said. How did she respond?

Josh
She said, "I can't answer that for you. But I can come alongside you to help bring clarity and perspective to your pain."

Beverly
Great answer! Now, emotional pain can make us question our mental stability. It throws us off balance. Yet, it's helpful for people to know that they aren't going crazy. They are experiencing life and sometimes life is hard to comprehend.

The 2nd point is specifically directed to those who are walking the road of grief. One thing grievers report is that what was helpful was being a part of a group where they knew they weren't going crazy.

Josh
Soon after Jenny died, I began attending a Grief Share group at Sycamore View. It was just a few of us in there, but words can't describe how impactful that group was for my grief journey. I can't remember all the lessons that were taught or all the conversations we had, but I can remember how people showed up and cared.

Beverly
I get to witness this every single week. Grievers come together, share life, and experience forms of healing. Every meeting we host is a glimpse of Heaven breaking into earth.

Josh
It's risky enough sitting with a therapist one-one-one. Yet you are talking about group therapy, which can be a whole different level of risk-taking.

Beverly
I know. It can be. Yet, it can be rewarding and healing. There is something powerful when we share something with others and the response is, "Me too."

Josh
Well, I know you aren't referencing the #MeToo movement, but I think it's worth noting that the reason the #MeToo movement (survivors of sexual abuse) grew to over 18 million people is because there was a connection made. People—especially women—had a story within them and the movement helped them know that they weren't alone.

Beverly
Exactly.
I spoke at a retreat a couple years ago. We played a game one night called "Circle of Friends." A woman would say something about herself, and if you also shared that emotion or experience, you would say out loud, "Same!"
For example, someone said, "Allergic to eggs."
Others yelled, "Same."
"Went to the principal's office in high school."
"Same!"
"Divorced by the age of 40."
"Same."
"Miscarriage."
"Same."

As you can imagine, it began fairly surface level, but it ended up being a powerful witness to the beauty of connection.

Josh
Mom, that is so powerful. There really is something transformative that happens when we know we are not alone. Without this connection, you can feel stuck. Life feels like you're stuck in quicksand and you can't move.

Beverly

That's it. You feel stuck. There are times people come to me and they feel stuck in grief. Sometimes people will ask, "Beverly, how do I know if I'm stuck?" My response is this, "When you find yourself looking backward more than forward. It's when you find yourself living in the past and not being able to move into the future."

Josh
Mom, one of the hardest things about therapy and healing is that once you commit to the journey to health, it may get harder before it gets better. Having to unpack pain in order to get to a healthier place may be challenging, but as one who has walked this journey multiple times, I can testify, it is worth every mile. It is worth every pain you unpack. It is worth every unhealthy emotion you have to face head on. It is worth every hurt that needs to be redeemed.

Beverly
It is a journey. For some of my clients, by the 3rd session, we aren't talking about the issue that first brought them in. We are talking about something else that their current pain or grief has awakened from their past. Therapy will do this to you. Grief events link.

Occasionally, when I'm facilitating retreats or grief workshops, I will have people write out a grief timeline. One time while leading people in this exercise, there was an eighty-year-old woman who kept writing, writing, and writing. It was that moment when you ask, "Put your pen down when you are finished," and there is that one person who just keeps on going. However, what was happening is this woman was noticing a thread in how she interpreted each of her events.

Josh
Grief events do link. As a reminder to our readers, when we discuss grief, we're not just talking about the death of a loved one. For me, I experienced a season of grief in 2010, 2014, and 2019. As we put the finishing touches on this book, we are twenty weeks into COVID-19. All of these grief experiences link. Though isolated events, there is a thread that holds them together. The thread is made known by our commitment to the journey toward healing.

Beverly
In this chapter, what I want people to know is this: Give yourself permission to ask for help. It takes courage to take the first step. Healing takes courage.

Josh

And I want people to know this: God is not only on the other side of healing, but God is on every step of the journey with you. Don't wait until you are hanging on by a thread to seek help. Take a risk. Make the call. Reach out. It could be the beginning of healing that could bear fruit for generations to come.

Chapter 16
Can Christians Go to God Angry?

Josh

When we first decided to write a book together, I knew I wanted to include a chapter about anger and disappointment. Now, this is kind of difficult, because I don't consider either of us to be angry people. Would you agree?

Beverly
Yes, I would agree with that.

Josh
It's not an emotion we tap into very often. Yet, when it comes to helping people navigate suffering, pain, and grief, it is an emotion that people aren't sure what to do with it. Would you agree with that?

Beverly
Absolutely! Here's an interesting fact about anger; it is not a primary emotion. However, it is a stage in the grief journey.

I work with women and men who do not know how to channel this stage of grief. Many people have been taught that "In your anger, do not sin," (Ephesians 4:26) really means, "Anger is sin." This is especially true when it comes to an emotion that enters into a prayer life. People aren't sure how to hold together faith in God and anger toward life. This is why I am glad we're taking a chapter to talk through this needed dialogue.

Josh
Over the years, I've had multiple people ask to meet with me in order to process their pain. I've had friends share with me that they feel anger toward God because of the cards they've been dealt in life, but they don't feel like they can talk to God about it.

My response is usually something like this, "Let me ask you a question. Do you think God can hear our conversation right now?
"Sure, I guess so."
"Do you believe that God is a faithful parent to us? In other words, do you believe God loves God's children?"
"Absolutely!"
"So, let me ask you this. If God can hear our conversation right now, and if God is a faithful parent who adores His children, what makes you think God's grace can't hold you through this honest, raw expression of hurt, pain, and loss?"
"Umm...well...maybe you're right."

Beverly

I love that! What a beautiful image of a loving parent welcoming honest expression from their children.

Leading up to this conversation, an image came to mind. I hesitated to tell this story, but I'm going to go ahead and tell it anyway. You've got to love when someone sets up a story like that, right?

Josh
HA! Right! Now I'm curious.

Beverly
My grandparents were raised in the country. When I say country, I mean deep in the country. My mom used to tell a story that when they would travel down a two-lane road, my great-grandfather would get out of the car to use the restroom. He would stand behind a tree, but the way he would position himself behind a tree was that he thought if he couldn't see you, you couldn't see him. It was like a little child playing hide-and-seek.

As funny as that image is in my head, I think that's what we do a lot. Ever since Genesis 3, we keep trying to hide. However, God sees us anyway. Sometimes, it's like we're hiding behind a tree because we don't want God to see what emotion we're experiencing in our lives, yet God is fully aware of it. So, quit hiding!

Josh
My first book, *Scarred Faith*, did not begin with me setting out to write a book. It began with me taking the season of Lent to journal every day. I needed space to process my own grief journey. Numerous emotions had grown inside of me over the first year after Jenny died, and I hadn't found an outlet to work through my questions and pain. I committed to journal five days a week for seven weeks. As I entered into that season, I sensed the Lord give me permission to process any emotion or question that was causing restlessness in my heart. The Lord was gracious to give me freedom. I took advantage of God's permission and invitation, and writing became my outlet. There was not an emotion I didn't take to God in that season. God didn't answer all of my questions, but God entered into the process with me, and that step on the part of God to enter into my pain provided just as much healing as answers would have given.

Beverly
Josh, this has been hard for me throughout my life. Anger was not an emotion I have ever been encouraged to feel; or to own. Shortly after Jenny died, a counselor friend

asked me why I wouldn't allow myself to get angry about Jenny's death. He asked it in a way as if to say, "You know anger is a part of grief, right? It's ok."

When he asked that question, I cried. I realized that I had skipped anger and had gone straight to disappointment. To say it bluntly, I wasn't angry with God as much as I was disappointed with God.

Josh
One of my all-time favorite authors is Philip Yancey. I have an entire row on my bookshelf dedicated to his books. Years ago, Yancey wrote a book called *Disappointment with God*. He would later reflect back on the criticism he received solely because of the title. I think he knew that the title would both cause some to lean in and others to stiff-arm. Yet, he went with the title anyway, because it explains what many people experience as they endure seasons of pain and suffering.

I've written about my faith crisis before. For me, I have never been through a season of doubting God's existence, but I have been through seasons where I have questioned God's intervention. When does God choose to intervene in situations, and when does God choose to keep His hands off? If we choose to live with high expectations of God, then there will be moments in life when we will feel as if God has let us down. We will experience seasons when we feel disappointed.

Beverly
Our other option is to live with low expectations of what God can do in the here and now. Yet, that doesn't lead to the kind of faith we have been invited into.

Josh
Exactly! Jesus didn't die, rise from the dead, and launch a movement for people to live with small expectations of what God can do. Jesus died to resurrect deep faith that our God can still do more than we could ever ask or imagine. And one day, God will do that. God will make all things right, Yet, as God waits for that day to come, there will be sorrow, and we will be left to navigate our way through it.

Beverly
Josh, one point I want people to hear when it comes to anger as an expression of faith: *stay curious*. I want to encourage people to stay curious in their emotions.

For some people, anger is what they feel, and it is where they choose to camp out.

I don't want people to camp out in anger. Own it. Feel it. Express it. But don't set up residence in anger.

Anger might be a step we take, but don't let it be where we stop. Go deeper. Anger is a secondary emotion that needs to reveal something else.

Stay curious!

Josh
I've also heard you talk about how we can be respectful in our anger.

Beverly
I often encourage my friends and clients to go to God with any emotion they may feel, but don't go to God disrespectfully. Be open with God. Be respectful too. God gets blamed for a lot of things God didn't do. Go to God, but be respectful.

Josh
That is such a good point!

The Psalms are a gift to us. I often encourage people to develop a spiritual discipline of reading the Psalms every day. I can remember you dwelling in the Psalms quite a bit when I still lived at home. It gave you prayer language. I would hear words, phrases, and expressions come from you that were embedded in your heart because you had immersed yourselves in this wonderful book.

The Psalms give us prayer language. They teach us to lay all we have in the presence of God trusting that God's faithfulness can carry us through it all. They teach us about honest, raw expression. It's the book Jesus drew from as he hung on a cross. Psalm 22 wasn't the place in Scripture he had read the day before in a quiet time. It was a chapter he had dwelled in throughout this life. It had become part of who He was.

Beverly
The Psalms have carried me through so many seasons in my life.

Josh
I often hear your voice reciting Psalm 63. I can't read it without hearing your voice.

Beverly
That Psalm has been healing for my soul. I still recite the first eight verses as my morning prayer.

The Psalms taught me to enter into the presence of God and to expect to be changed.

I think that's where I would like to end this chapter; no matter what emotion we take before God in prayer, expect to be changed.

God has no desire to leave us in our anger. God intends to transform it into an expression that will ultimately change the world.

Truth!

Josh
Truth!

Chapter 17
"I Know Exactly How You Feel"

Josh
Mom, you and I are always up for a good story, right?

Beverly
Absolutely. Always. With me, whether I'm telling them or hearing them, it is always story time.

Josh
Let me begin with a story as we engage in this next dialogue.

Toward the very end of my Master of Divinity program, we were assigned a project in which we needed to explore our metaphor for ministry. It was a short project that required pastoral imagination. I had colleagues who chose metaphors like symphony directors, coaches, and midwives. I chose to explore and unpack the metaphor: *crossing guard*.

At the time, Kayci and I lived next to a four-way stop by an elementary school, and every single school day, I witnessed a crossing guard doing their job. It didn't matter if the weather was scorching hot, freezing cold, or pouring down rain, the crossing guard was in their place doing their job. As I reflected, one thing I appreciate about crossing guards is that they walk with people through the intersections. They don't pat them on the back when it looks clear and wish them luck as they attempt to make it to the other side. They don't stand on one side of the street and wave people over when it seems like cars have come to a stop. They walk with people through the intersections and crossroads.

This is how Jesus revealed to us the heart of God. If you want to know what God is like, look at Jesus. Jesus doesn't stand on the other side of eternity and wave us to Him, and He doesn't pat us on our backs in our baptisms and wish us good luck in life. Jesus walks with us through the intersections. It doesn't matter what the elements are like or what season of life we are in, Jesus walks with us through it all.

John 1:14, "The Word became flesh and moved into the neighborhood." (The Message). As I think about how we come alongside others in their pain, this metaphor comes to mind. What Jesus does is what the church is called to do as well. We engage, walk with, cross intersections alongside of, and join others as we walk through life.

Beverly
When I think of the people who have meant the most to me as I navigate my own journey, it's the people who keep showing up. They keep walking with me. I get to see this metaphor played out in *Jenny's Hope* every single day. We don't pat others on the

back and wish them luck and we don't wave people over to the other side. We walk with people. I love this metaphor! In fact, I'm pretty sure you got it from me.

Josh
Ha! Probably so. Very few of us have original ideas.

Let's talk about the phrase, "I know exactly how you feel."

Now, before we unpack this phrase, I feel like we need to emphasize a point we have made throughout this book multiple times. You and I do not want to make people so nervous about phrases we use that they choose to never say anything because they don't want to say the wrong thing. However, we do want to encourage people to weigh their words. Know what you mean when you say certain things.

Beverly
That is very well said. I'm begging people to not choose to be silent. Take risks. Be present with people. Use words. Yet, weigh them. Most of our words come from hearts that want to do good. We mean well.

Josh
Sure, we do.
So, let's talk about this phrase: *I know exactly how you feel.*
Neither of us choose to use this phrase. Let's explain why.

Beverly
I've had numerous clients who are traveling painful journeys reflect on this statement by saying, "How can you know what I feel when I don't know how I feel?"

Josh
Many stories are similar, but no one's story is the exact same. There is a connection that can be made between people who journeyed through divorce, or have overcome alcoholism, or have survived sexual abuse, or between parents who have lost a child. Yet, every story is unique.

Beverly
For one fellow griever, this phrase was their throat-punch statement. We all have those statements that when spoken, we want to offer up a jab. For her, this was it. She told me that someone once spoke this statement to her early on grief and she came

unglued. She said, "Really?!?! You think you know exactly how I feel? My child died of a heat stroke. He literally boiled to death, yet you want to say that you know exactly how I feel?"

This phrase is an attempt to make a connection, but sometimes it can create distance and a lack of empathy.

Josh
So, help us, mom. What language do you use to let people know there is a connection as two people walk through life? You do a lot of speaking, equipping, and coaching in the grief world both at *Jenny's Hope* and as you travel throughout the world, so help us know how to make a connection.

Beverly
Here are two ways I equip people in this area:

1. **Don't anticipate what others feel**. Every story is unique. There are stages of grief, and we all move through those stages at different paces. One person may be in the denial stage for six weeks, while someone else moves through denial in a day or two. Don't anticipate. Stay curious. Allow others to feel their way along the journey.
2. The phrase I often use and equip others to use is this, "**My heart is joined with yours as we journey together.**" There are multiple ways to express that there is a connection made through walking painful journeys. Explore phrases that keep us curious and unique.

Josh
I love that statement: **My heart is joined with yours as we journey together.** Exploring ways to express connection while also acknowledging that each person's story is unique can generate healthy dialogue and meaningful moments. I think it is also worth acknowledging that such an approach lends itself to storytelling. As we stated at the beginning of this conversation, you and I are big on storytelling.

Beverly
This was extremely meaningful to me in my pain. I treasured—and still treasure—times people let me sit and tell stories. I also love hearing other people tell theirs.

There are times at Jenny's Hope, or when I'm with others that they'll begin telling stories, and they'll ask, "Oops. Have I already told you this story?" I've learned to immediately respond by saying, "You know what? You have told this story. But I want to hear it again. Keep going."

Instead of saying, "You already told me that," respond with, "Please tell it again." Especially for grievers, this is a way of keeping their loved one's stories alive.

Josh
I love this so much! Let me tell you about a time I did something very similar.

I spoke at a staff retreat for another church one weekend a couple years ago. During one of our sessions, I had the team share stories about pivotal moments in their lives that threw their rhythms off. One woman shared that just recently her daughter had completed suicide. It was tragic. When the session was over, I immediately walked over to her and took a seat. Most of the team had moved into another room for snacks and drinks. After sitting down, I said, "Will you do me a favor? Will you tell me a story about your daughter's life that would give me a better feel for the kind of woman she was?" Her face lit up. She began telling stories.

I don't know what led me to approach the conversation the way I did. Maybe it was you, Mom, having equipped me over time on how to walk with others. I didn't feel the need to say, "How did she take her own life?" I wanted to know about her as a person.

Beverly
I've heard you share that story before, and that's exactly what I want to do for others. Grievers have stories to tell. They need to know their story is unique, because God has made them unique. Stay curious. Don't anticipate. Come alongside others. Walk with people through the intersections.

I hope something in this chapter has equipped our readers to live intentionally.

Chapter 18
Does God Cry?

Josh
This chapter is a conversation about emotions, so I thought it would be fun to begin with this: Which of your three children made you cry the most growing up?

Beverly
Tricky! Tricky! You're funny! Most of my tears over you three as adults have been from overwhelmingly deep joy. But I shed tears when our vacations and holiday times come to a close. There was also the time when you … Just kidding!

Josh
I'll take your "just kidding" as a wink. Ha!

A few months after Jenny died, I was asked to give a keynote (a main session) at a conference hosted by a Christian university. After each keynote message, the speaker walked to the right of the stage and took a seat with the director of the event where they proceeded to have a five-minute Q&A based on the content of the message. During the ensuing dialogue, people were offered the opportunity to text in questions.

As we took our seats, I glanced down at the front row. You and dad were there, as well as Aunt Barbie, and of course, Kayci. I noticed that Kayci was making a motion to me. She held up two fingers as if to make a "V," and proceeded to bring them together. A couple of minutes went by before it dawned on me that I chose to take a very casual posture as I sat down in my seat. My legs were wide open. Kayci was attempting to tell me to close my legs. Kayci would later say, "I know you had on khakis, but no more crotch-shots when in front of crowds."

Beverly
Joshua Louis Ross!

Josh
Uh-oh. You just said my middle name. It's never a good thing when you use my middle name.

Beverly
I remember that moment. I was thinking to myself, "Joshua Louis, I taught you to have better posture than that."

Josh

As I changed my posture, the director read a question that a college student had texted in. It was only three words, but they are three words that have stuck with me now for over a decade.
"***Does God cry?***"

Beverly
Hum. Wow. I do remember that.

Josh
After a pause, my response was an emphatic, "Absolutely!"
In this conversation for this chapter, I want to share why I answered the way I did, but before that, I'm curious about how we view emotions in our current culture. Now, I get that how people think about tears in 2020 isn't the same as 1920, but how many times do people cry in front of you, and immediately begin apologizing for their tears?

"I'm so sorry, Josh. I did not plan on crying today."

"I'm so sorry, Beverly. I told myself I wasn't going to cry in your office today."

Beverly
Oh, my goodness. All the time.

Josh
What do you say? How do you respond?

Beverly
I say, "In this room tears are welcome." That's my go-to line.

Josh
That's a better line than what I usually use. Typically, my response is to say, "I don't accept your apology. I'm honored you would trust me with what is going on in your life."

In all seriousness, it's difficult for me to remember a time when someone cried and didn't apologize.

Beverly
It is evidence of how much we struggle with vulnerability. To cry is seen by many as a sign of weakness.

Josh
Talking about weakness, how about this one? How often have you seen someone walking a road of grief and state how they need to be strong for those around them? Or someone gave another advice by saying, "You need to be strong for your kids?" Or, "You need to be strong for your parents?"

Beverly
Unfortunately, all the time. Again, we need to help dispel the notion that showing emotion is a sign of weakness. It's not. Sometimes, that is exactly what the rest of your family needs to witness. They need to see us vulnerable, authentic, and living in the moment.

Josh
So, we know we have emotions, but, what about God? Does God cry?

When I think about this question, my mind and heart go to a few places in the Bible. The second half of Revelation 21:4 states, "There will be no more death or mourning or crying or pain, for the old order of things has passed away." Does this remind you of a song that used to be sung in our churches?

Beverly
Oh, yes! "No Tears in Heaven." It was a fairly upbeat song.

Josh
(First verse)
No tears in heaven, no sorrows given
All will be glory in that land
There'll be no sadness all will be gladness
When we shall join that happy band.

(Chorus)
No tears (in heaven bear) no tears (no tears up there)
Sorrow and pain will all have gone
No tears (in heaven bear) no tears (no tears up there)
No tears in heaven will be known.

Beverly
It was a catchy tune. We sang this song all the time when I was growing up.

Josh

I'm not knocking the song. But it only touches on the second part of Revelation 21:4.

Beverly
Exactly.

Josh
Do you remember how Revelation 21:4 begins?

Beverly
I do. It's a declaration.
"God will wipe every tear from their eyes."

Josh
This was mind-blowing to me a little over a decade ago. The same verse that tells us that there will be no tears in heaven also tells us that God will wipe the tears from faces.

Beverly
We serve a tear-wiping God.

Josh
I can't tell you how meaningful this was to me. I use it in funerals, counseling sessions, and when I'm sitting with people who are grieving the loss of a marriage, a job, or a dream. God wipes tears from our faces.

So, according to Revelation 21:4, heaven has tears, and God knows exactly what to do with them.

Beverly
It reminds me of Hebrews 5:7, "During the days of Jesus' life on earth, he offered up prayers and petitions with fervent cries and tears to the one who could save him from death, and he was heard because of his reverent submission."

Josh
Now, I feel like we're beginning to preach. I'm loving it.

Beverly
Truth!

Josh

Hebrews 5 is one of a few places that refer to Jesus expressing emotion. As we've said throughout this book, if you want to know what God is like, look at Jesus. Jesus experienced a lot of different emotions, and sadness was one of them.

Mom, let me ask you this, have you ever had someone just call and cry with you? Or when you cried in the presence of someone else, they just let you cry?

Beverly
I have. There are times you have done this for me. I have friends who have let me cry around them, and their posture didn't change. They didn't become uncomfortable. They didn't change the subject. They didn't joke their way out of the conversation. They just sat there.

Josh
It shocks people sometimes, but when they cry around me, not only do I not try to fix it, but I treat them in the moment as if what is happening doesn't need to be fixed. Emotions are a release, and sometimes, that's exactly what needs to be done.

Okay, Mom, there are two other places in the New Testament where Jesus cries. Can you name them?

Beverly
I can definitely name one. It's the shortest verse in the Bible. John 11:35, "Jesus wept." Help me with the other one.

Josh
That's ok. I know I'm putting you on the spot in front of hundreds -- or hopefully thousands -- of readers.

It is Luke 19:41, "As Jesus approached Jerusalem and saw the city, He wept over it."

Beverly
Oh, yes! I know that verse has meant a lot to you as you've ministered in Memphis.

Josh
It was huge for me. Within my first year, God used Luke 19:41 to cultivate a deep love for the 901. The fact that Jesus would weep over a city, knowing He was within a few days of laying down His life so others could have life, inspired me to work to do the same. I want to learn to weep over the brokenness around me, and then work to lay

down my life and resources so others can have life. It's also a call for the church to do the same.

Ok, Mom, hang with me here. Did you know there are two different Greek words that are used to describe the way Jesus cried?

Beverly
I was not aware of that. Keep going.

Josh
This is where I could say anything I want, try to make it sound smart, and you probably won't know if I'm telling the truth or not.

Beverly
I trust that you'll do the right thing.

Josh
Ha! I've heard those words all of my life. "Josh, I know you'll do the right thing."

Beverly
The words, Josh. What are the Greek words?

Josh
Dakruo means to shed tears. This is what Jesus does in John 11:35. It's also the word used in Hebrews 5:7. Jesus shed tears.

Klaiw means loud expression of grief. This is what Jesus does in Luke 19:41.

I'm not attempting to elevate one form of tears over the other. If anything, I'm trying to point out that there were multiple different ways Jesus allowed tears to flow in his life. In John 11:33, Mary and Martha "dakruo." They let out loud expressions of grief. Their brother had just died. Why would they do anything different? Jesus responds to their grief by shedding tears (klaiw). He enters into their grief. In Luke 19:41, Jesus dakruo's. He sees rebellion, lack of urgency, shallow faith, and hard hearts, and he lets out loud expressions of grief. Jesus was desperate to see the world set right, and He knew what it was going to take to get it done.

Beverly
Just hearing you unpack that makes me celebrate that this is what our God is like! This is who our God is.

Josh
That's right. This is what our God is like.

Let me ask you this, Mom, when you cry, how do you think God responds? What is God doing when God sees you shedding tears?

Beverly
I sense the Lord comforting me. I sense God's compassion and mercy. I'm a child in the arms of a loving Father. I don't think God is disappointed at all.

Josh
I don't think God's disappointed either. In fact, I think there are times when a tear might fall from heaven, while at the same time a hand reaches to wipe a tear from our cheek. This is what our God is like.

Beverly
Tucked away in the Psalms is this verse I had skipped over for years of my life. Yet, over the past decade, it has taken hold of my heart in profound ways. Psalm 56:8, "You have kept count of my tossings; put my tears in your bottle. Are they not in your record?" It's this powerful image of our tears being collected.

Josh
What a powerful image!

Beverly
But that's not how it ends. The very next statement is this declaration, "Then my enemies will retreat in the day when I call. This I know, that God is for me."

Josh
Oh wow! So, in a way, our collected tears become a witness to all those around us that God is on the move. That'll preach!

Beverly
It will preach. It will also inspire us to live.
Our God enters into our pain.

Josh
God's grace gets lower than our lowest low.

Beverly
And the day will come when God will wipe all of our tears away, and all things will be right.

Josh
Amen!

Beverly
Amen!

Chapter 19
How Can I Be a Faithful Friend to Someone Who is Grieving?

Josh
Mom, we have come to the end of our dialogue. I hope this has been helpful for all who have joined us on the journey.

Beverly
From the moment you pitched the idea of having a conversational section to our book, I loved it. I believe in the power of helpful dialogue. I know we chose ten conversations, and we could have included dozens of other topics, but I hope that what we have discussed has equipped others to be faithful companions on the grief journey, whether it is their own story that caused them to join the journey, or someone else's.

Josh
If we come to the end of a meal while sitting at a restaurant, this is where we choose whether we're going to eat dessert or not. We've enjoyed the food, the conversations have been engaging, and now there are just a few more things left to say. I'm curious, when you and dad eat out, do you order dessert?

Beverly
Hardly ever. However, there are a few restaurants that we know going in, we are definitely getting dessert at this place!

Josh
What's your favorite dessert?

Beverly
Hands down, crème brûlée.

Josh
No way! That's mine too! Well, that and banana pudding.

Beverly
If crème brûlée is on a menu, there's a good chance I am getting dessert.

Josh
Mom, we want to end this section by helping people be faithful friends as they journey with others through pain. This may seem a little scattered, but that's ok. We want to

help people think and we want to give people practical things to do. We want to do this without making it sound like, "Here are the five steps you need to follow to be a good friend to others who are hurting." Every person, situation, and season of life is different.

Beverly
We wrote this book because we want to help people. We want to use our wisdom and experiences to equip others to live intentionally and with purpose.

Let me begin with this, one of my favorite grief experts is Dr. Alan Wolfelt. In his book *Companioning the Bereaved*, he talks about the gift of companioning. It's the best way to walk with people through grief. We intentionally and strategically choose to *companion* well. This means we refuse to allow ourselves to see others as projects to be fixed, or problems to be solved, but as people to be loved. This means we resist the urge to rush others through grief. *Companioning well* means we make a long-term commitment to come alongside others, and to willingly choose to move at their pace.

Josh
It sounds like you are describing what many have called "the ministry of presence."

Beverly
That's exactly what it is. We come alongside others, and sometimes we may use words. But we can always offer our presence, even when we don't have something to say. There is something courageous and powerful about saying, "I am here. I don't have all the answers. I can't make pain go away. But I can keep showing up."

Josh
It's one of the most meaningful gifts we can offer others.

Beverly
Absolutely, it is!

Every Sunday after Jenny died, an elder's wife at church would approach me and say, "Beverly, what do you want me to pray?" There was something about how she asked the question that was so genuine, inviting, and welcoming. It was her way of asking me what the cry of my heart was that week, and by how I answered, it was her way of joining me in my cry. It made me get intentional about what to ask for.

Josh
I've been through a few rough seasons in life and ministry over the past decade. Each time, I have friends who wanted to be with me, and they allowed me to set the tone and agenda. If I wanted to talk about the painful journey, they were all ears. If I wanted to just tell stories, or talk about sports, or just hang out, they would do it.

Beverly
I think it's also worth sharing that I do have a few people in my life, who are incredible listeners, but they aren't afraid to challenge me too. They push me. They ask hard questions. However, they are people who have earned my trust and the right to speak deeply into my life. We need those friends.

Josh
I have a few of those friends too, and I can't imagine where my life would be without them.
Mom, we often live in the tension that life has us in. Sometimes the way I say it is like this: There are times when how we walk into the future with God isn't going to be like how we have walked in the past with God. It's not necessarily because God has changed, but because life has changed. Learning to navigate seasons of pain can feel like we are stuck in the unknown.

I have a good friend who shares about the day his daughter passed away. The same day, in the same hospital, their good friends were giving birth to a child. Now, think about if you were friends of both of these families and you were in the hospital visiting them that day. You would walk onto one hallway where there was the sound of new life. There was joy, excitement, and wonder. Then, you would take the elevator, walk onto another floor where a mom and dad were saying goodbye to their baby girl. It was a day in which joy and sorrow met.

Beverly
Talk about living in the tension.

Josh
I remember Philip Yancey once referred to a story of a man who was in the hospital after a terrible accident that left him paralyzed from the waist down. While lying in the hospital bed, they would set a timer for thirty minutes, and each time the timer would go off, they would roll him over on his other side in order to prevent bedsores. For thirty minutes, he stared at a wall where a picture hung of the birth of Jesus. It was Mary holding a newborn. Then, they would flip him, and he would stare at another wall that had the crucifixion of Jesus. One moment, he was in awe of the fact that God

would enter into this world in human flesh. Jesus came to dwell with people. Then, he would look into another picture soaked in pain, offering up the same question Jesus did on the cross, "My God, my God, why do you forsake me?"

Beverly
Talk about being suspended between life and death. There is so much in that image to unpack.

Josh
I know, right! A phrase I've often used in my preaching is this: *in the unknown, God dwells*.

Beverly
TRUTH!

Josh
I used that phrase when I spoke at the Gulf Coast Getaway in Florida a few years ago. A few days later, I received a message from a young woman who attended the event who took the liberty to go permanent with the phrase, *In the unknown, God dwells*. She had it tattooed on her forearm.

Beverly
I can say that I've never responded to a point in a sermon by getting a tattoo, but that's a great story.

Josh
Sorry for digressing.
Here's how I want to encourage our readers: Commit to living in the tension with people. Live in the unknown with others. God does some of God's best work in those places. God's not just at the destination. God is on the journey.

Beverly
There are many lessons I learned from Jenny. One is that Jenny used to give gifts to friends of index cards. There were times she gave blank cards, and she would encourage people to write out Scriptures on them to encourage others on their faith journey. However, I also discovered that there were times when Jenny would give index cards to people that already had Scriptures on them. She had taken the time to write out specific promises of God for people struggling through a specific season in life. It was her way of saying, "When you don't know where to start. When you don't know how to take your next step. Let this be your guide."

Josh
Small things with great love.

Beverly
In the summer of 2010, Rick and I had planned a trip to travel to Scotland. Then, Jenny died. I was hesitant to still travel because of the timing, but grateful we went. As you know, Rick's family has Scottish roots, and Rick loves golf.

Josh
Oh, yes, I know. I like telling people that we had kinfolk fight next to William Wallace. I'm not sure if it's true or not, but it could have happened.

Beverly
That's like us telling people that we are related to Kenny Rogers, which is true, but it's not like we ever met him.

Back to our trip. We connected in London and hopped onto a smaller plane that was going to carry us to Glasgow. That's when we met up with another couple. His name is H.L. When he saw me, the first thing he said was, "Flip flops? Are you really going to wear flip flops on this trip?" It was cold where we were going, but I like to travel while being comfortable.

Then, he said this, "When you want to talk about Jenny, we want to hear. When you don't, we don't have to. You tell us when you want to talk."

I have carried those words with me for years. It gave us permission. It made us feel loved. It gave us space. Needless to say, the trip was great, and the fellowship was exactly what we needed.

Josh
I'm sure it is stories like what you just told that have equipped Kayci and me over time. Our good friends, Kevin and Sarah Campbell, called us in March of this year and informed us that Sarah had breast cancer. We cried. Since then, we facetime every couple of weeks with them, and Kayci and I tell them, "We want to move at your pace. If you want to talk about treatment and chemo, we'll talk about it. If you want to share stories about how we used to stay up until 1:00 a.m. together eating cookies and telling stories, we will. We just want to be here for you."

Beverly
Choosing to walk with people takes a lot of grace, and a lot of risk. Grace that we will mess up. And risk, that we've got to keep trying.

But we can do this.

Friends, you can do this.

Choose today to *companion well*.

Epilogue
Stepping into the Arena
(Beverly)

We come to the very end of this book. It has been quite an adventure. I don't know if you've made it this far in just a couple of days, or maybe your reading pace took you a few weeks to get here. Though we come to the end of a book, most of you are reading as wounded and scarred people, because you have lived life. You need to know that I think you're brave. You are still standing. You may walk with a limp, but I'm so proud of you for still walking. Coming to the end of a book isn't coming to the end of life. We want to leave you with encouraging words that will equip you on this journey.

In 2016, Rick and I led a trip that followed Paul's second missionary journey. While in Rome, we visited the Colosseum, a place so thick with history you can almost hear the battle cries of the gladiators. There are rooms under the arena floor where the prisoners were held until it was time for the clash. When their names were called, they walked the stairs into the arena knowing that there would be blood and possibly death. Those who made it out alive were taken back to the rooms underneath the stage to prepare for the next battle. Their focus was survival.

Shortly after Jenny's funeral, I texted Rick Atchley, a good friend, to ask if he thought Jenny's death was part of a spiritual battle. Rick responded, "I don't know if Jenny's death was an attack by the enemy, but I do know there has been a battle since the day of her death."

My name had been called and I was in the arena. I knew there would be blood. I knew there could be death. What was at stake wasn't my body, but my faith.

***

At the very end of the book of Ephesians, Paul tells us how to prepare for the inevitable - spiritual warfare. We have to stay prepared, not in a fearful way but in a ready way.

I found myself turning to Ephesians 6 not only to remind myself of the prep work I needed for the next battle, but also for direction on how to get back up and stand following this attack. I had to *dig down deep* and *remember* the basics of my faith as the Spirit poured warm oil into the gaping wounds in my soul in order to keep the infection out.

What Paul wanted for the churches in Ephesus is what I want for you. I want you to be prepared and equipped for the battle we are in as we journey through life.

***

When Jenny was going into seventh grade, my sister invited us to go to church camp for a week. Barbie and her husband, Cecil, were in youth ministry and we always had a blast together, so I said yes! Who wouldn't give up sleep and good food for a week to hang out in the woods with a group of hormonal teens?

One afternoon early in the week, we were walking to the lake to swim when I tripped. It was a simple fall. I stood up, brushed the gravel and sand off my knee and resumed laughing at whatever story was being told. When we got to the lake, I washed my knee off in the swimming area. This was also where the teenage girls washed their hair and shaved their legs, and where teenage boys claimed to take soapless baths. The water was nasty but if you just didn't think about all that, it felt good to cool off.

The next morning, my knee was so gross, and it hurt to walk. Infection had set in. I will spare you the details that are making me squirm as I recall the scene. The camp nurse took one look at my knee and began to gather supplies. She would have to scrape away the scab that was already forming to put medicine directly into the wound. I visited her two to three times a day until the infection was out and the scab could form over a clean wound.

Scabs form best over clean wounds. Clean wounds make better scars.

In her book, *Jesus Calling*, Sarah Young writes, "Wounds that you shut away from the light of My love will fester and become wormy."[26] I needed the basic ointment of the light of God's love to clean out my wounds after Jenny's death so a scab could form to make a better scar, a scar I would carry forever.

A Scarred Hope.

When I first began writing this book, I already knew the title would be *Scarred Hope*. But every time I typed it, my fingers wrote Scared Hope, only one "r." Jenny's death brought a raw fear into the depths of my soul, but by following Paul's guidance in Ephesians 6, I found an intensely strong scar forming where my fear had once been. Grief required more bravery than I could've ever imagined. Bravery to live.

---

[26] Sarah Young in *Jesus Calling*, July 28 (Nashville, TN: Thomas Nelson, 2004), 219.

***

Paul ends his letter to the Ephesians by preparing them to march into the world. For Paul, it wasn't a matter of *if* believers marched into the world, but **what to wear** as they went. Faith encourages people to keep moving and keep going. Paul didn't wish them luck or ask the church to stay inside locked doors and to play it safe, but to properly equip themselves for engagement.

Paul writes:

Finally, be strong in the Lord and in His mighty power. Put on the full armor of God so that you can take your stand against the devil's schemes. For our struggle is not against flesh and blood, but against the rulers, against the authorities, against the powers of this dark world and against the spiritual forces of evil in the heavenly realms.

Therefore put on the full armor of God, so that when the day of evil comes, you may be able to stand your ground, and after you have done everything, to stand. Stand firm then, with the belt of **truth** *buckled around your waist, with the breastplate of* **righteousness** *in place, and with our feet fitted with the readiness that comes from the gospel of* **peace**. *In addition to all this, take up the shield of* **faith**, *with which you can extinguish all the flaming arrows of the evil one. Take the helmet of* **salvation** *and the sword of the Spirit, which is* **the word** *of God. And* **pray** *in the Spirit on all occasions with all kinds of prayers and requests. With this in mind,* **be alert** *and always keep on praying for all the saints.*[27]

As a child, I was taught that Paul strategically placed each piece of the armor in its precise location. But when Jenny died, I was so desperate for each piece that I didn't care where it was placed. I just wanted to make sure I had the **full** armor.

My friends, I'm pleading with you to armor up. Paul was writing to wounded, scarred, hurting people. These were folks with all forms of immorality in their past. Yet, Jesus wasn't through with them. And Jesus isn't through with you. Armor up. One piece at a time.

Truth.
Righteousness.
Peace.
Faith.

---

[27] Ephesians 6:10-18.

Salvation.
The Word of God.
Prayer.

***

TRUTH.
At the end of 2004, Rick was fired from a church we had been serving less than two years. We believed we were equipped to help this unhealthy church, but they weren't ready to receive help. This was a hard season for both of us. Church-wounds are included in the list of grief-producing events.

Shortly after the firing, I was at lunch with another counselor when she began asking me questions. My response to every one of her questions was, "I don't know."

There are two words I don't want used with my name in the same sentence - pessimist and boring. Having the same answer to every question placed me at high risk to sound boring. So, I changed my voice inflection:

"I don't know."
"I DON'T know."
"I don't KNOW."

Can you hear the difference?

"Where are you going to live?" "I don't know."
"Is Rick going to stay in ministry?" "I DON'T know."
"What are you going to do professionally?" "I don't KNOW."

Oh, there were lots more.

Suddenly, I felt my throat clamp tightly. Oh no! I was about to start squeaking - that squeak right before the really big fit comes - the all-out ugly cry. We were in a nice restaurant with quiet conversations going on around us, so it seemed inappropriate to start wailing at our table. I quickly said my good-byes, telling my friend I would call her soon.

I barely made it to my car before the tears erupted. I cried out to the Lord, "Please, Father, tell me something I know. There are so many unknowns swirling around me."

The Lord spoke into my soul. It was not a male voice, but it was profoundly settling. God told me the three things that I can KNOW.

1. My daughter, I will always be God no matter what happens to you.
2. You are coming to see my face.
3. You have a close circle of family and friends who will journey beside you until you get here. Outside of these, you know nothing. You just get to pretend like you do.

In the confusing days of grief, these were on replay in my mind. Knowing truth is part of the armor of God. His truth is more truth than my truth. Know what you know, even when your faith is limping.

RIGHTEOUSNESS

Righteousness means living in the grace of Jesus. It also means doing what's right. It surprised me how important this would be in my grief journey.

When I was down on the arena floor, struggling to get back up, the evil taunts were loud. His taunts included a rolodex of memories filled with guilt and shame.

What did I do wrong to make this happen? What did I miss? Why didn't I finish that conversation? Many of my clients ask these same questions. Was it a past sin being punished? Was I not good enough to have a baby? Am I unlovable? Is that why she left?

***

Guilt and shame? Those words are defined very differently. Guilt is recognizing that I did something wrong, something I wish I hadn't done. Guilt can be from the Lord and is His redirection of misguided steps as He, simultaneously, fills us with hope that we can do better.

In some of our grief stories, we have to wrestle with our guilt. We struggle with the deep desire to have just a few seconds of time back so we could make life-saving changes. Listen to me. If you were in my office right now, I would stretch out to hold your hands in mine as I tell you that I firmly believe we are doing the best we know how to do in this moment and that we were doing our best in *that* moment too.

We have to release these taunting memories to the One who knows more about the stories than we have a clue.

But shame is different. Shame is the belief that I not only did something bad, but I am bad. It is not rooted in behavior, but in a lack of intrinsic value. The worst thing about shame is that it is void of hope. Shame adds heavy weight to the grief journey. Please seek help from a professional counselor or spiritual director if you are stuck in a loop of shame.

***

What does righteousness have to do with preparing for spiritual battle? Or what is its role in forming a scar from the last wound? We learn to view our history from the grace of Jesus. We learn to view our present in the smallest of steps, asking what is the next right thing to do? Don't look a week down the road or even a day. Just take the next right step.

Know that righteousness protects our hearts.

PEACE
I had not been able to read while Jenny was in the hospital. My brain felt like mush. About eight weeks after her death, I decided to try to read the book of Job. Job and I had never been great friends, but I felt like the timing was right. Job knew suffering and I wanted to know what he knew.

In Job 1, there is a mystery encounter between God and satan. A wager takes place. Every time I read this story, I feel like I'm seeing an extremely private scene, one I'm not supposed to be watching. God gives permission for the powers of darkness to make Job suffer, but He sets boundaries around how deep the torture can go. God trusted Job as His Exhibit A for faith.

I wanted to see this familiar story through fresh eyes, so I chose Eugene Peterson's The Message. At the end of Chapter 3, these words struck my soul: "The worst of my fears has come true, what I have dreaded most has happened. My repose is shattered, my peace destroyed. No rest for me, ever -- death has invaded life."

I closed that big book with a loud thud. "That's exactly right, Lord. I don't have peace. I have never known a season void of peace. But now, I agree with Job. It's gone."

The Lord responded, "Ah, my daughter, that is Job speaking from His place of pain, but you have the Holy Spirit living inside of you. Where My Spirit is, there is peace."

"Open the eyes of my heart, Lord, I don't miss one glimpse of Your peace." That has become my constant prayer.

Since that moment on my porch, I have not had another day without peace. I receive it in glimpses, in the smallest of moments. I receive it in sweeping gestures, grand moments of awe-filled encounters. But, mostly His peace is in my breath. One breath at a time.

Peace rejuvenates what is healthy in us so that our wounds can heal.

FAITH

Eighteen months after Jenny died, I was speaking in West Texas, driving down I-20, when my eyes were drawn to a parched field, devastated by a wildfire. It was gray ash, filled with deep crevices. I wanted to walk on that ground. I wanted to touch the ash, sifting it through my fingers. But I was running out of gas and I knew I didn't have enough gas to make a u-turn and go back.

When I pulled in at the gas pump, I grabbed my journal and wrote: *Death created for me a spiritual earthquake and left me sifting through the rubble to find the remnants of my faith.*

***

You've seen those stories on the evening news of a family walking through what once was their comfortable home, picking up what's left, after a horrible fire. "Oh, I remember this..." They are digging through the destruction to find the reminders of what once were their treasures. The wedding portraits. The baby clothes. The photo album. Could they be salvaged?

And sometimes that's what I had to do when a fire ripped through my heart. I was forced to search for the remnants of my faith. God's history with me had been rich and deep. God has been faithful. I did not want to walk away from Him. Those memories with Him are my treasures. Could they be salvaged?

Faith is not faith if there aren't doubts. Faith is a choice of direction. The response to our faith matters, not only on earth, but in the heavenly realms.

As Jesus was about to be arrested and killed, He had one more supper with the boys to prepare them for what was to come. I love His words to Simon Peter, telling him what He is praying for him and giving him direction:

"Simon, Simon, Satan has asked to sift you (plural) as wheat. But I have prayed for you Simon, that your faith may not fail. And when you have turned back, strengthen your brothers."[28]

Jesus could have prayed that His disciples would be kept safe physically, that they would live long lives of ministry to tell His stories. But He didn't. He prayed for their faith. When a life is lived with faith, its length becomes unimportant in the hands of the Living God.

SALVATION

I was speaking out of town once when my GPS took me to an empty field with five minutes to spare before I was supposed to step onto the stage. I sat there for a minute staring at the tall grass blowing, waiting for a church building to appear any second. I panicked until I remembered I needed to recalibrate my destination. Destinations matter, especially when a group has gathered, waiting on us to show up. When we are in Jesus, Heaven is our destination. There is a group gathered, waiting for us to join them.

When someone close to us dies, our own deaths become a reality. It isn't helpful to live so focused on our deaths that we forget to focus on *how* we live. Our salvation is not only our *where*, but it is our *how*. And this "how" creates unspeakable excitement, with a heavy measure of anticipation. Knowing we are saved changes the way we live, not just what happens when we die.

Death is not the worst thing that can happen. Dying without Jesus is. We have to recalibrate our destination. There are no empty fields when Heaven is in view.

***

Here is a short excerpt from a piece Jenny wrote for her 31st birthday party, her last birthday on earth. You can hear her excitement and now it has become mine.

She hosted a blessing party where she spoke words of affirmation over her close friends and family. She went around the room and gifted each of us with words of blessing.

---

[28] Luke 22:31-32.

She started with me, "Mom, you are my hope-giver. You have given me hope to have a healthy and devoted marriage. You have instilled in me a hope for what is to come."

She ended with words of blessing over her little girl, "'You are snazzy. You stand up for yourself, love God, love your family and friends, love reading your Bible. You have a desire for everyone to know Jesus. You have a compassionate spirit. You are my greatest gift and most special thing to celebrate! When you were born was when I learned what prayer truly meant! I knew I had to have it to be the mama that you deserved!"

Here is the powerful conclusion:
"I praise you God that you have blessed me with this specific cloud of witnesses!! I am so favored by you for giving me them! It makes me want to fall back into your arms and take this huge sigh to know when I die it is many of these girls that will greet me and be the forefront to your glory in Heaven and that maybe they will even be the ones to vocalize to me and step aside to reveal my Savior!! As they beautifully and angelically say, "Jenny, this is Jesus! And for those that pass after me, It will be such great days in heaven to welcome them in and to give them some of their first heavenly hugs and kisses!
God, You are good. You are perfect. You are truth! You are the One we all claim to live and breath for. Thank you for celebration! I love you, Jesus!"

I want to live like I know where I'm going, and like I'm excited to get there! I cannot wait for Jenny to introduce me to Jesus! I will run to Him first and then she and I will jump up and down for years.

THE WORD

Paul calls the Word the sword of the Spirit. It's our best weapon to fight against the confusion. But grievers report that it is also confusing to see so many words on a page. And where on earth do you start reading in this huge book we call the Bible?

A few years ago, I had been praying for a friend who didn't know Jesus. One day, while I was on a Florida beach, she texted to tell me that after reading Josh's first book, *Scarred Faith*, she had downloaded her first Bible. After a moment of excitement, I went into a small panic. If she starts at Genesis, Numbers is coming before she can get to Jesus! I hurriedly text her, "John is Rick's favorite book and Luke is mine. Read one of those."

Always start with Jesus. God-in-flesh. The One who walked on dirt. The One who felt everything we feel; including heartache. Start with one verse at a time about Jesus.

***

Friends, we need to have verses written like graffiti on the walls of our hearts, ready for battle. We may encounter a season when reading becomes difficult. May we speak to one another in "psalms, hymns, and spiritual songs."[29] It is in them that we find Hope.

"For everything that was written in the past was written to teach us, so that through the endurance taught in the Scriptures and the encouragement they provide we might have hope."[30]

PRAY
In historical movies, battle scenes begin in postures of power, maybe on a horse with spears lifted high or with running warriors screaming at the top of their lungs. When there is something scary to be done, it matters what we do with our bodies. Amy Cuddy, a body language researcher from Harvard, went viral in 2010 when she introduced us to the magic of the power pose. You know the one where your hands are on your hips, feet are squared up under your shoulders, like Wonder Woman. That pose is said to increase testosterone (feelings of power) and decrease cortisol (stress). I've been on platforms with women who get into this pose before they walk to the podium to speak publicly.

Some people rank public speaking as the thing they fear most. I once did too. When I was a little girl, I had a speech impediment. I stuttered. I believed because my words stuttered that my brain might too. I was terrified to make a comment in class, much less hold a microphone. Then the Lord invited me to teach - publicly, on a mic. He also taught me that I would need a power pose. It consisted of being on my knees with hands lifted to Him or flat on my face before Him, remembering that He is my source of power. I don't need power. I need empowerment.

Grief brought me much more fear than public speaking. I didn't have many words to pray, but I had my pose. I committed to never pray, or sing, with my arms crossed in front of me or with my hands clasped behind me. I committed to pray with open palms, sometimes facing down or sometimes facing up. I love Richard Foster's approach: Keep palms down when you're laying things at the feet of Jesus or at the

---
[29] Ephesians 5:19.
[30] Romans 15:4.

base of the cross. Keep palms up when you are asking to receive from the Lord. Sometimes I pray with arms reaching high to let Him know that I am wanting to be held, or with palms up to tell Him how great He is.

I have a morning ritual that is also a power pose. I sit on the side of the bed and picture the Lord inviting me to rise up: "Good morning, my daughter, I've got some work for you to do today."

I pause as I picture the Lord putting spiritual braces on my knees. He steadies me for the day ahead. My knees are so weak but this reminds me of my total dependence on the empowerment of the Spirit alive in me. When my steps stutter, He braces my knees.

Prayer is the battle cry of a spiritual warrior!

BE ALERT
When our family gathers, there is an unspoken tradition that continues to surprise me. I will be talking to one of our sons, usually in the kitchen, when his eyes glance behind me. Depending on the depth of conversation, it can take me a minute to catch on. The other son is sneaking up behind me. The ritual is that they try to tickle me, and I beat them off with my flip flops, or the nearest spatula. It always happens. It always catches me off guard. And I always vow to be more prepared the next time.

This is where we come to the end of our journey together. Ephesians 6 wasn't the end of the story for the churches in Ephesus, and it's not where our story ends either.

In Ephesians 6, Paul tells us to be alert and be ready. There will be attacks and the powers of darkness want to catch you distracted, off-guard. He keeps attacking in the same way over and over and we keep falling for it. The death rate is still 100%. Broken relationships and broken bodies are all around us. Every person has a story of pain and suffering. It is part of the human experience. God prepares all of His children to suffer.

And that, my friends, means we prepare for war.

The enemy is clearly defined, and it is not each other. We do not bully each other. We support each other. We do not call anyone names - any one. We show grace and mercy and love. We stand together and whisper words of truth.

Jesus is fighting for us. Jesus is fighting alongside of us.

We treat one another right, not because of who they are, but because of Whose we are.

We practice Romans 12:18, "As far as goes with you, live at peace with everyone." That is right in the middle of Paul advising us how to treat our enemies. We have too much of the Spirit's peace internally that we can't help but express it externally.

We look for people who need to be reminded of the reason for our faith, our hope.

We whisper, "The tomb is empty" to each other.

We remind ourselves that we are on a path to see the Victorious One, our King.

We allow His Word to be our light and we pray, with boldness, for our faith. Our prayers are more about our faith than our physical health. Because that is what matters more than anything.

So armor up!

Together, we never take our eyes off of Hope! Even when it is a Scarred Hope.

ACKNOWLEDGEMENTS

BEVERLY WOULD LIKE TO THANK:

Sally Rodgers. Thank you for taking on the challenge of editing a first-time author and her much more experienced son. The Lord prompted me to ask you after our first lunch together, and I am delighted you agreed. I am grateful for your patience and your encouragement. Your honesty pushed me to dig deeper. Your calming presence was exactly what I needed. I appreciate your ability to recognize my overuse of exclamation marks and quotation marks. Thank you, Josh, for pointing those out! Quotation marks I can do without, but I do love an exclamation! Sally, thank you!

Casey Kleeb. When Josh asked me if I knew a graphic artist who could help us with the book cover, your face was the only one on my radar. You have a gift for hearing my heart and finding an artistic expression with beauty and sacred space.

Jenn Ross. Thank you for reading every word, even when it wasn't very good yet, and for being excited with me as ideas formed. Your excitement over my writing built excitement in me to continue to write.

Kayci Ross. Thank you for your encouragement and giving me a safe place to discuss hard stuff over the last ten years.

Jonathan. You have a gift for making me laugh and relax. I am grateful for every song you have sent me that speaks of Hope, Joy, and beauty from ashes. They have filled me with bravery.

Barbie. I'm grateful that you are my sister and my built-in best friend. I'm grateful for our shared histories and our shared love for our families.

Rick. I am so grateful to have you as my walking companion for every step of this journey. Thank you for covering me in prayer and for helping me find quiet spaces to write. Thank you for speaking truth into my insecurities and for listening to me work through ways to express my heart on paper. I love you!

The Board of Directors at Wise County Christian Counseling (Derrick Boyd, Matt Fisher, Shelly Harrison, Teri Houchin, Dan Mallory, and Susan Parks). Thank you for your faithful support and encouragement to make my dreams a reality.

Britt Sanders. Thank you for protecting my calendar and for reading the manuscripts. Your friendship is a blessing.

The staff at WiseCCC. You form a beautifully skilled team. I'm grateful for your professionalism and for your friendship. You rock!

Devon McCain. Thank you for saying "yes" to when I asked you to be our coordinator for *Jenny's Hope*. The gifts you bring are invaluable. I'm grateful for your partnership in this ministry and for your friendship. And I love the way you say the word "beautiful!" It is inspiring.

Jenny's Hope volunteers. You are the heartbeat of this organization. Thank you for facilitating, for organizing, for bringing food, and for being willing to do anything else we ask of you to support grieving children.

Susan Parks and Dede Diaczenko. You are both so talented! Thanks for sharing your artistic gifts with us to make our building, especially *Jenny's Hope*, warm and inviting. I'm grateful you could hear my heart even when I couldn't find the words.

My clients, members of our grief groups, Jenny's Hope participants. Thank you for sharing your stories with me. I will treasure them always.

The churches who have invited me to share our story. I love the army of friends I've made during our times together. Thank you for hearing my heart and for asking deep questions.

Many friends have sat with me for hours and hours, allowing me time and space to process my pain without judgement or correction. You heard my stories over and over. Your eyes held my heart with tenderness as I explored my faith. You prayed with me and reminded me that the tomb is empty. Jesus used each of you so well to gently encourage me to cling to Him. I'm afraid to try to name you, but I'm praying the Lord will nudge you as you read this, and you'll just know it was you.

Josh. I am deeply grateful for your invitation to write with you. It was a dream for me. Your advice and guidance pushed me forward. You taught me how to incorporate writing into my everyday life and still find time to sleep. This project never would've been completed if not for your experience and mentoring. Yes, I have loved being mentored by my son. I've learned so much from you! It has been a joy!

JOSH WOULD LIKE TO THANK:

Mom, thank you for saying yes to this project. You have always been an inspiration to me. To partner with you in this effort has been one of the greatest joys of my life. We did it!

Kayci, I love what we have together. No matter how hard life is sometimes, I'm able to live with joy and perseverance because I know you have my back no matter what.

Truitt and Noah, I had no clue being a dad was going to be so much fun. I am able to protect you from some forms of pain in life, but I also know that I am unable to protect you from it all. I can only hope that your mom and I have helped to build a solid foundation for you to stand on. Jesus is for you. I can't wait to see how God continues to raise both of you up to be a force for good in the world.

To Luke Norsworthy, Josh Graves, Chris Seidman, and Rick Atchley, thank you for your friendship. You are a safe place for me. I appreciate every trip, meal, text thread, and conversation we have together. Especially over the past couple of years, your friendship has sustained my faith and life in ministry.

Kevin and Sarah Campbell, Kayci and I are Campbell fans for life. You have modeled faithfulness in the face of adversity. Sarah, Kayci and I are so honored to call you a close friend.

David and Lisa Fraze, you have modeled how to have a no-matter-what-kind-of-faith as well as anyone I know. As Kayci's youth minister growing up, I get to reap the benefits of the fruit of your ministry every single day of my life. You both poured into my wife during the most formative years of her life. You taught her how to have a radical, obedient, persistent faith. Thank you! David, you have become one of my closest friends. What have we not talked about over the past few years? I love you both!